25 LESSONS LEARNED

IN 25+ YEARS IN CATHOLIC SCHOOL DEVELOPMENT

Written by Frank Donaldson

Second Printing 2016

Published in the United States of America by the National Catholic Educational Association.
www.NCEA.org

ISBN 978-1-55833-603-2
Part No. DEV-70-1557

This book is dedicated to the memory of
Dr. Michael E. Guillot (1953 – 2015),
a true Catholic school visionary leader and the
contributor to many shared beliefs and core values
of Catholic school development.

TABLE OF CONTENTS

SECTION A: INTRODUCTION

Understanding the History of the Lessons Learned in 25+ Years

It was 1986 when I was first introduced to the word *development*. Back then, most Catholic schools were trying to balance their budgets on tuition, subsidies and fund-raisers. Most were making it, but there was a new feeling in the air – change was coming. Facilities were getting older; the number of religious still teaching in Catholic schools was dwindling; demographics were shifting; technology costs were just beginning to hit the spreadsheets; teacher salaries were increasing; enrollment was beginning to be a challenge in certain areas of the country. The "glory days" of Catholic schools were beginning to fade. What were the answers?

For many, the answers were to keep doing the same old thing – add more fund-raisers, take in unqualified students, hire the least expensive faculty/staff members, band-aid the facility issues, tighten the budget and cut certain programs and activities. The list goes on, and unfortunately, still exists today in some areas.

The administrators at the school where I was working in New Orleans, Louisiana decided that the above approaches were not for them. They opened up a development office and hired a development director. Because it was so new at the time, the main emphasis was on public relations – creating newsletters and alumni bulletins, putting ads in the newspaper, sending out press releases, and running calendar sales. That worked for one year, and then change was needed.

And so, in 1987 – 1988, I was hired as the new Development Director at Mercy Academy in uptown New Orleans – an all-girls school that had been around for many, many years. For 20 years I had taught English, journalism, theatre arts, and coached a little basketball in Catholic schools throughout south Louisiana. What did I know about *development*? The first thing I did was register for a week long workshop put on by Catholic School Management; it was held in Orlando, Florida. For five days, I sat there and listened and absorbed and listened some more. I learned a lot, but I came away with one really good feeling – I could do this because I had done it before, and back then I did not even know what I had done was called *development*.

From 1980 to 1986, I directed a musical group in New Orleans called CELEBRATION! This was an "Up with People" type of group made up of high school and college men and women who danced, sang and played music for thousands of people throughout the south. We ended up performing over 150 shows for the 1984 World's Fair in New Orleans. We had over 100 cast members, and in order to sustain ourselves we had to promote, publicize, raise money, write grants, costume, equip, and develop a base of people who would support these young people and their musical endeavors. We even recorded two albums and sold those. In some form or another, I had been down the *development* pathway. I now had to apply it to Catholic schools.

The first year was exciting, because we implemented many new processes – a new mission and vision statement, a vibrant "student recruitment" effort built around bringing prospective students on campus, an Annual Fund Drive, an Alumnae Association, a phonathon, a Hall of Fame, a quarterly newsletter, a Strategic Plan for Development, and a major donor outreach. That first year we engaged over 400 people into our *development* efforts, and it was right then that I realized that the true definition of *development* made perfect sense: *Development is the meaningful involvement of people in your mission and vision for the future.*

The *development* efforts continued along for the next few years, and we had much success, thanks to so many people who became involved. *Belonging does lead to believing.* In 1988 I was asked to "consult" with some area parishes and schools who had heard about what we were doing at Mercy Academy. That was the beginning of my consulting career, although part-time. In 1989 I decided to "hang out my shingle" and the Institute for School and Parish Development (ISPD) was begun.

The last 25+ years have been exciting and rewarding. I have had the rare opportunity to work with hundreds of Catholic leaders all across the country in over 50 dioceses. Bishops, superintendents, pastors, presidents, principals, development directors, marketing directors, board members, volunteers, faculty and staff members, and so many more. There are so many outstanding leaders in Catholic schools. And so, after hundreds of consults, hundreds of workshops and seminars, and hundreds of campaigns and planning processes, here we are, 25+ years later and with over 2,000,000 miles logged in on Delta and Southwest Airlines.

I would like to share some of these experiences with you in this book. I believe these lessons can save you some time and spare you some walks down pathways that do not lead to the best results. I have learned a lot in 25+ years, and so it is from this perspective that I would like to offer these 25 lessons.

Twenty-Five Year History of Catholic School Development/Advancement

When I first got involved in Catholic school *development* in the '80's, there were already some key leaders who were paving the way for our schools – Sister Kathleen Collins, Sister Mary Burke, Father John Flynn, Richard Burke, and a few others. In fact, on the cover of one of the issues of *NCEA Notes* in 1990 was the title, *Development the Key to Catholic Schools' Future*. Yes, back then it was called *development* and not *advancement*. We referred to attracting new students as *student recruitment* and not *enrollment management*. Very few elementary schools were doing anything with *development*, yet more and more Catholic/private high schools were seeing the value of hiring a person as their Development Director. One of the most revealing documents that was produced in the late '80's was a chart developed by Father John Flynn titled "Development vs. Fund-Raising." It was and is an excellent visual that shows the short term impact of a fund-raising event culture as opposed to the long term impact of a *development* approach.

ISPD was in the minority back in those days with our ways of thinking. Even though some Catholic leaders emphasized people involvement, for many pastors, principals, finance councils and board members, *development* did equal fund-raising, and yet ISPD defined the word as meaningfully inviting and involving people in order to better develop the school for the future. Today, the same can be said about the word *advancement*. We believe it is all about advancing a Catholic school to be the very best it can be, and that is done through attracting and nurturing the many, many resources that are available.

Today, most Catholic high schools have a Director, and more often than not, that person is referred to as the Director of Advancement, although some Catholic high schools continue to refer to that person as the Development Director. NCEA leans more to the word *advancement* for secondary schools and *development* for elementary schools. From our experience, there are still many Catholic elementary schools that do not have a Development Director. Through the years, the names have evolved, many taking their lead from higher education. From what I have observed, the religious community-owned schools have taken their lead from the universities; the diocesan-owned Catholic high schools have taken their lead from the religious community-owned schools; the Catholic elementary schools have taken their lead from the Catholic high schools; and the parishes with Catholic elementary schools have realized the value of a *development* effort when their schools have been successful – hence the rise of parish/school *development* efforts.

I have little doubt that the names will keep evolving as we continue to discover the best language to use to explain and describe our *development/advancement* efforts.

What's in it for the Reader?

There were many times in these past 25+ years that it was tempting to take the easy way out and not say a word when we observed Catholic school *development* efforts being centered on direct mail, e-mails, fund-raising events and development directors sitting behind computers all day writing newsletters, inputting into Excel spreadsheets, and applying for grants. Plus, it was hard when working with pastors or principals or presidents and having to say what they were doing needed a total re-engineering or re-structuring. Thousands of hours of discussions, meetings, cups of coffee – all have led to this point where we now have the experience to write about it. There have been mistakes made; there have been processes that could have gone better; there have been situations that could have been handled differently, and that really is the purpose of this book – to share with you, the reader, those lessons that we know, after 25+ years, do work and are successful. Hopefully, these lessons will save you many hours of time and will take you in a direction that will produce wonderful results. That is the purpose of this book.

Core Values

Throughout the past 25+ years, ISPD has remained a small to medium size Catholic consulting firm – by design. We are driven by seven core values:

- A commitment to our Catholic faith;
- A commitment to exclusively serving Catholic institutions;
- A commitment to integrity in our company culture;
- A commitment to customized consulting and teaching;

- A commitment to building teams;
- A commitment to helping foster a belonging and affirming culture in Catholic institutions;
- A commitment to meaningfully engaging people.

Understanding the Terminology

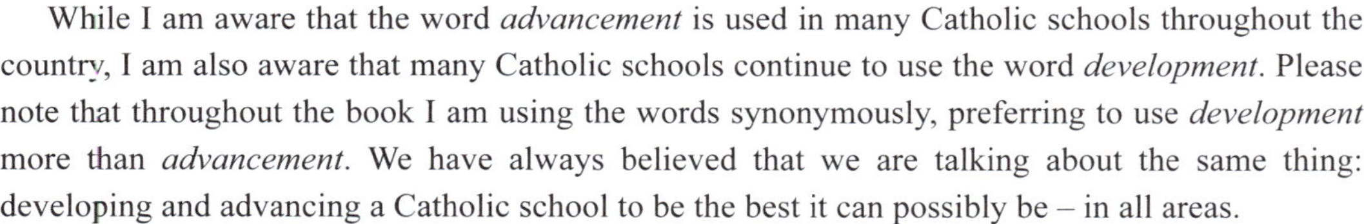

While I am aware that the word *advancement* is used in many Catholic schools throughout the country, I am also aware that many Catholic schools continue to use the word *development*. Please note that throughout the book I am using the words synonymously, preferring to use *development* more than *advancement*. We have always believed that we are talking about the same thing: developing and advancing a Catholic school to be the best it can possibly be – in all areas.

SECTION B: PHILOSOPHY AND FUNDAMENTALS OF CATHOLIC SCHOOL DEVELOPMENT

Lesson 1: Promote the Involvement of People as the Common Denominator of Your Catholic School Development Efforts.

One of the major challenges Catholic school leaders face is educating their key internal publics (faculty, staff, parents, students, board leaders, alumni) on the meaning of the word *development*. Closely associated with that is the constant struggle to have Catholic school leaders understand that *development* is a process and not a program that is plugged in at various times when money is needed. Too often we have heard the nightmare stories of a development director hired and then fired after one year because all the school really wanted was a full-time fund-raiser to run the fair, the festival, the auction, the bingo, the golf tournament, and/or the calendar raffle sale. And, because the administration and school board did not understand Catholic *development*, everything was judged on the amount of money raised.

We define development as ***the meaningful involvement of people in the school's mission and vision for the future.***

By the very definition of the word, *development* takes time — usually 2-4 years — before a Catholic school will begin to see substantial results. School leaders must be willing to invest money in order to make money and build a trusting faith community.

We have searched for ways to educate and inform Catholic school leaders about the *development* process, and over the years, we have developed an approach to teaching and in-servicing. We call this approach: ***The 7 "I"s of the Catholic School Development Process.*** (***See** 7 **"I"s Chart***)

- ***Identify:*** To continually *identify* the people who could become key to *development/advancement* success;
- ***Inform:*** To reach out to all publics (parents, alumni, past parents, parishioners, grandparents, businesses, the overall community, feeder sources, etc.) and *inform* them of the vision, case, and the "WOW points" of your Catholic school;
- ***Invite:*** To have the above publics take a closer look at you and you at them — usually through personal *invitation* vehicles such as input sessions, surveys, interviews, cup of coffee meetings, planning sessions, questionnaires, listening sessions, etc.;
- ***Involve:*** To meaningfully *involve* and engage people in the *development* processes such as strategic planning, annual fund leadership, marketing council, alumni association, parent ambassador team, business community council, etc.;

- ***Implement:*** To *implement* the plans, the strategies and processes that have been created through the involvement of people;
- ***Invest:*** To invite people to *invest* in the future of your Catholic school by seeing themselves as true "stewards" of that school;
- ***Improve:*** To set up *development* processes that will be continually enhanced through a Total Quality (continuous *improvement*) approach.

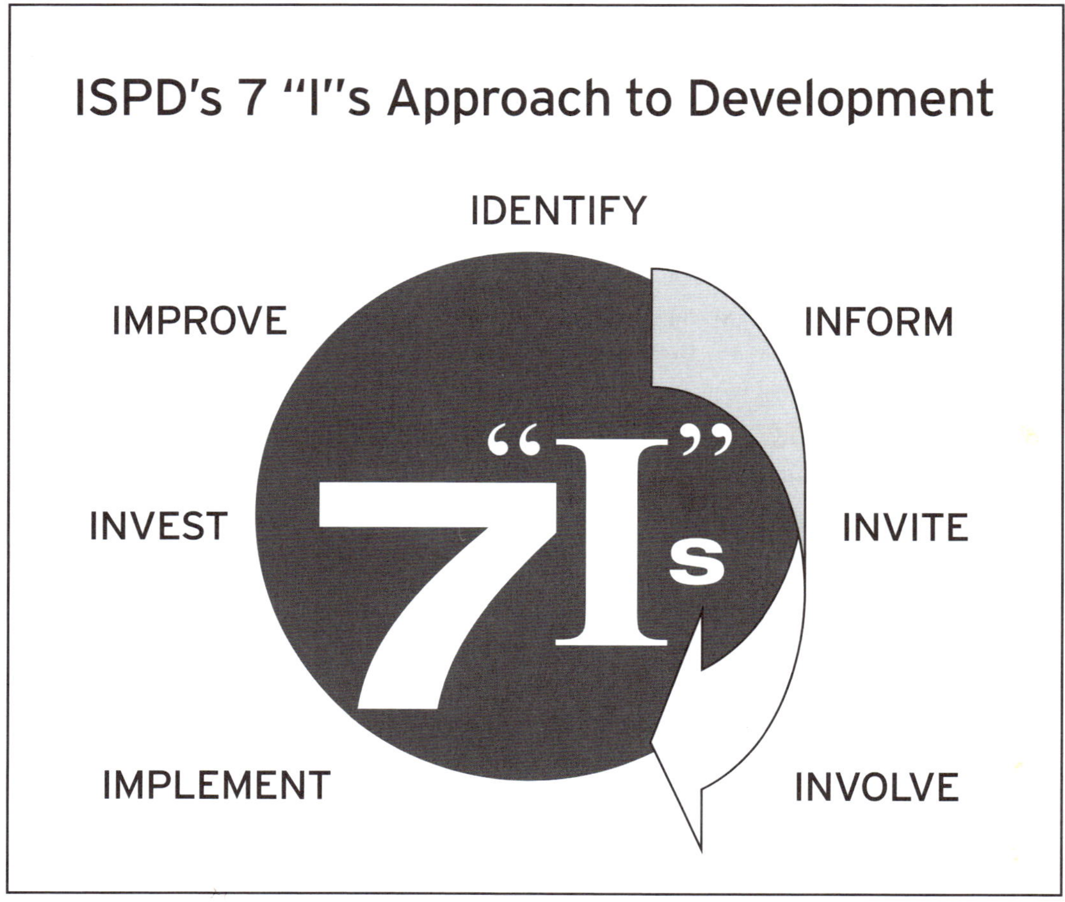

It is essential to understand that the first four "I"s mainly refer to people and the last 3 "I"s refer to processes. Please do not think that with the first I — *identify* — that we are talking just about identification of people with money. This is not a program approach where everything is in a neat little box; this is looking at *development* in terms of a system of inter-related parts that all must function together in order for the entire system to be successful.

Also, this is not a process that will take place in one year, or two, or three. Based upon the last "I" — *improve* — it will be necessary to take a continuous improvement approach to your *development* processes and realize that we are talking about a cycle of always getting better.

Every year it will be important to prioritize what is important for your Catholic school at that time and concentrate on implementing the key pieces in that stage of the 7 "I" cycle.

Catholic school *development* is an exciting and dynamic process -- when implemented correctly and when it is built around the engagement of people. For some Catholic leaders, this has been a real challenge. We usually illustrate this with our *ripples in the pond* illustration. (***See Chart below***).

If a pebble is dropped into a pond, we say that the first ripple could represent those 25 people in a Catholic school who are always there, always volunteering and taking on leadership roles. They are the backbone of the school and strongly believe in the mission, the leadership, and the direction. Unfortunately, many burn out and eventually leave – some even hanging on for an extra year or two because of control.

There is a second ripple of people, however, and this usually represents 50+ folks who would love to get involved but they do not, and it is usually because of one reason – no one ***personally*** invites them. Plus, there are third and fourth ripples of people (parents, past parents, alumni, grandparents, community members, etc.), and we do not even know anything about them. This is why we say that the number one challenge facing Catholic schools today is not raising money, is not bringing in more students, and is not building new buildings. The number 1 challenge facing Catholic schools is to create the avenues, roadways, and vehicles to invite, involve and engage people in our mission, vision, and dynamic plans for the future.

Oftentimes, we will challenge Catholic school leaders to invite and involve 100 new people into their schools every year; this book will articulate many ways that this can be done. It is as important to measure our success by the number of people we engage as it is to measure our success by the amount of money raised. Indeed, this is a people business, and the more we get our hearts fixed to give personal invitations rather than receive money, the more we will advance and develop our Catholic schools.

Possibly, one of the best lessons on giving was written with the stub of a pencil on two sides of a sheet of wrapping paper which had been folded and placed for protection in a tin baking powder can. The can had been wired to an old pump which offered the only chance of water on a very long and seldom used trail across the Amargosa Desert. This is what was written:

> *This pump is all right as of June 1932. I put a new sucker washer into it and it ought to last five years. But the washer dries out and the pump has got to be primed. Under the white rock I buried a bottle of water, out of the sun and cork end up. There is enough water in it to prime this pump but not if you drink some first. Pour about ¼ and let her soak to wet the leather. Then pour the rest medium fast and pump like hell. You'll git water. The well has never run dry. Have faith.*
>
> *When you get watered up, fill the bottle and put it back like you found it for the next feller.*
> *(Signed) Desert Pete*
>
> *P.S. Don't go drinking up the water first. Prime the pump and you will git all the water you can hold. And next time remember that life is like this pump. It has to be primed. I've give my last dime away a dozen times to prime my pump, and I've fed my last beans to a stranger. It never failed yet to git me an answer. You got to git your heart fixed to give before you can be give to.*

Lesson 2: Remember That Everything Begins with Your Mission, Vision, and Core Values.

In the Spirituality Series, Henri J.M. Nouwen talks about *A Spirituality of Fundraising*. For so many years, we have stayed away from using the word *fundraising* to equally define Catholic *development*, *advancement* and/or *stewardship*; however, in *A Spirituality of Fundraising*, Nouwen clearly elevates the word *fundraising* into a much wider view and articulates what we have always believed. We really are talking about developing and advancing our Catholic schools.

Development/advancement is not a response to a crisis, even though that may be the starting point for some Catholic schools who decide they need to hire a development director or put on a fund-raising event. *Development* is a ministry.

To quote from Nouwen, "(*Development*) is, first and foremost, a form of ministry. It is a way of announcing our vision and inviting other people into our mission. Vision and mission are so central to the life of God's people that without vision we perish and without mission we lose our way (Prov. 29:18; 2 Kings 21:1-9). Vision brings together needs and resources to meet those needs (Acts 9:1-19). Vision also shows us new directions and opportunities for our mission (Acts: 16:9-10). Vision gives us courage to speak when we might want to remain silent (Acts 18:9)."

The reason we say that Nouwen's view is much wider than how many define *fundraising* can be seen in this next passage. "When we seek to raise funds we are not saying, 'Please could you help us out because lately it's been hard.' Rather, we are declaring, 'We have a vision that is amazing and exciting. We are inviting you to invest yourself through the many resources that God has given you – your energy, your prayers, your talents, and your finances – in this work to which God has called us'. Our invitation is clear and confident because we trust that our vision and mission are like 'trees planted by streams of water, which yield their fruit in its season, and their leaves do not wither'." (Ps. 1:3)

After all, as we have said for 25+ years, *development*, *advancement*, and *stewardship* are all about inviting people to share the resources that God has given them and through that sharing we are able to develop and advance our mission and vision. With this thought, here are some questions for us to ponder:

- Is our mission statement clear and compelling (and short) and does it state the constant purpose of what we do day to day?
- Do we have a vision that can be clearly articulated in the spoken and written word that shows the dynamic direction our Catholic school is headed?
- Do our mission and vision create a compelling case for why people should share their resources and become involved with us?
- Are all of our key messengers (pastor, president, principal, faculty, staff, councils and boards, student leaders, parent leaders, and alumni leaders) sharing the same vision and mission (messages)?

- Are these messages collectively agreed upon by all of the messengers? (In other words, is there a unified effort by all messengers to create and share our mission and vision?)
- Is our vision unique, distinctive, and exciting to share?

For some of us, perhaps it is time to revisit our mission and see if our vision is relevant, compelling and exciting. Maybe it is time to pour our new wine into new wineskins, for as Nouwen says, "Vision gives us courage to speak when we might want to remain silent."

Lesson 3: The Life and Viability of Your Catholic School Continues with Your Leadership.

When I first started the company in 1990, I "hung my shingle" out in an office building on St. Charles Avenue, right across the street from The Pontchartrain Hotel – in the Garden District of New Orleans. The price was great for a 1200 square foot office, mainly because the owners were going to be tearing the 10 story building down in 2-3 years. It was at that time that I really got to know two people who helped shape the mission, philosophy, and core values of ISPD – Michael Guillot and Ken Murray. Ken owned a marketing company down the hall from our office, and Michael and I teamed up with some consulting contracts – mainly because I had run out of time, and he had such a vast knowledge of Catholic school *development*.

All three of us agreed that Catholic *development* was all about building relationships and involving people, so as we created and designed planning processes, capital campaign strategies, enrollment management initiatives, annual fund campaigns, stewardship efforts, marketing plans, and more, we built everything around that theme: *Development is the meaningful involvement of people in your mission and vision for the future.*

In the first year of full time consulting, one of the clients that Michael and I were working with was a parochial school that wanted to create a long-range plan for all areas – *academics, Catholic identity, faculty and staff, student life, athletics, administration and finance, development and marketing*, and *buildings and grounds*. They also wanted to build a stronger bond between the parish and the school. Our work started out with an assessment that we conducted; then it led to the formation of a Core Team, and then on to setting up the planning process with over 75 people involved. After 3-4 months, everything was going well, and we moved to the first Parish/School Planning Session – a 7:00 PM – 9:00 PM meeting in the Parish Life Center. We introduced the process, got people placed into the proper Planning Area Team, and were ready to dismiss so the small groups could start their work. All of a sudden, the pastor stood up and said, "Folks, before you go to your teams, I do want to make an announcement." All the participants stopped in their tracks. He went on to say, "I realize that all of you are here to plan for many things with our school, but let me say one thing. Regardless of what you come up with in your planning sessions, in two months this parish will be launching a $5,000,000 campaign to build a new church. I know I haven't said anything to anybody about that, but that is what we will be doing."

Needless to say, what the pastor had to say took the wind out of everyone's sails. That was not the reason they had signed up for the four meetings; that was not what they had bought into; plus, no one in the parish – including parish and finance councils – had any idea that this was coming. To make a long story short, a number of people left – not only the planning process but also the parish. After another six months, the pastor was replaced.

This was a valuable lesson that we learned in the first year of the company. In many, many cases, the effectiveness of a Catholic school can be traced back to two words: leadership and attitude. I have often said that effective leaders in a Catholic school demonstrate and live out five principles:

1. They build relationships – eyeball to eyeball and person to person. They understand the value of a belonging culture.
2. They can clearly -- and with excitement -- articulate the future vision for that Catholic school, a vision that has been created through the meaningful involvement of people.
3. They believe in teams. **T**ogether **E**veryone **A**chieves **M**ore.
4. They cultivate a collaborative culture – one that seeks input and respects the opinions of others, one that builds trust and confidence in and among all who work with the school to build it stronger.
5. They are accessible and interesting. True leaders take the position that others are doing them a favor by reaching out and sharing their ideas, and because of that, true leaders make themselves available. They study and experiment and are not afraid to be innovative; they seek their own niche in the Catholic school world. They are not willing to settle for status quo and have their school be like every other Catholic school in the diocese.

One of the most interesting studies on leadership was written by Dr. Michael E. Guillot. His dissertation – *The One Less Traveled By – A New Model of Leadership for the Non-Profit Sector* – is both informative and mind-provoking. (http://aura.antioch.edu/etds/165) As mentioned earlier, Michael was instrumental in helping me start this company over 25 years ago. Unfortunately, on Sunday, April 12, 2015, Michael passed away at his home in New Orleans after a brief battle with cancer. Catholic school education lost a true champion and a powerful visionary leader. Michael had served in Catholic schools as an English teacher, development director, assistant principal, and principal – for a number of years and in several different schools. Over those years he had carved out an excellent reputation, and as his life moved onward, he began to evolve more and more into the world of Catholic School Development – just about the same time that I was heading in that direction. I knew back then that Michael was special; he was cut from a different cloth than other people I knew in *development*. Many others I had come in contact with would always talk about the money and how much they had raised in an annual fund or how they had asked for their first million dollar gift. I never heard that from Michael. What I did hear was a genuine belief in people, a passion for the mission of the institution with whom he was consulting, and a desire to always think beyond the norm, beyond the boundary lines that kept everything so safe and normal.

In 2011, my alma mater, De La Salle High School in New Orleans, launched a search for a new president. Like many Catholic schools going through change, they needed an innovator and a leader who could take them beyond the norm and do something very special. I had the wonderful pleasure of working with the board president and the search committee; Michael Guillot was our answer. He and I spoke several times about the situation at De La Salle in the earlier months of his tenure. I always knew he was the right man at the right time in the right position. He was deep into his PhD dissertation on non-profit leadership, delving into a topic and promoting a dissertation that was extremely innovative. He knew how to listen; he knew how to bring people together and make them feel special; he knew he needed to create that culture of belonging; he knew he needed to continue to instill the La Sallian charism and philosophy; he knew he was not "the man" – that he was mainly an instrument for change. He, and other leaders at DLS, created four classrooms of the future. He worked with many to change the culture into one of trust and caring. Everything he taught at the university level after Hurricane Katrina in 2005, all of the themes of his doctoral work, all of the years he spent "cutting his teeth" on what made institutions great – all of this came into focus at De La Salle High School in New Orleans. In just three short years, he led the school's transformation from one that was struggling with its identity to a school that continues to be on the cutting edge of innovation today. Enrollment has increased by over 25%. The curriculum has skyrocketed in creativity. Michael brought in some of the most outstanding Catholic educators, coaches and administrators in this area of the south to be part of the team. They continue to build and grow. Michael laid the foundation.

Like many, I was shocked when I heard about his health and later shaken when learning of his terminal condition. I was very fortunate over the last month of his life to be able to visit with Michael several times and talk with him about this book. As I told him several times, he is as much a part of these lessons as anyone; we learned many things together. In my last visit with Michael, we went over the chapter highlights, and he ended up sharing the transformational steps that have taken place at De La Salle High School in the past three years. It is quite amazing that so much has transpired at the school in such a short period of time; however – like the old days – we both agreed that many times it often comes down to two words – leadership and attitude.

In his dissertation, Michael proposed ten building blocks of nonprofit leadership (10BB). To frame those ten building blocks, he created four domains – the ***Personal Domain, the Organizational Domain,*** the ***Communal Domain,*** and the ***Global Domain.*** (***See Building Blocks Chart***)

In the ***Personal Domain***, Michael proposes four dimensions: *purpose, knowledge, courage* and *appreciation* (Guillot 62). He defines *purpose* as ". . . the possession of a clear direction for both the leader and the organization she or he will lead" (Guillot 62). He uses *knowledge* to ". . . suggest the aspect of leadership that engages in meaningful inquiry and seeks information and wisdom to enhance leadership behaviors"(Guillot 62). He says, "personal *courage* suggests a moral strength to persevere and to withstand fear" (Guillot 62), and, ". . . *appreciation* describes the personal aspect of leadership that is affirming, positive, and nurturing in dealing with those they lead" (Guillot 62).

In the ***Organizational Domain***, Michael maintains that three building blocks make up this level of the pyramid: *vision, adaptation, and relationships*. "The presence of a *vision*, some sense of potential future state that is compelling and shared, is a necessary part of leading a nonprofit organization" (Guillot 62). He goes on to say that "the ability to *adapt* creatively within the dynamic environment of our sector links effectiveness with imagination" (Guillot 62). The third building block in the Organizational Domain, once again, goes to heart of this company's mission and to the core of what Michael and I discussed hundreds of times. "An organization is formed for the purpose of establishing and sustaining meaningful *relationships*. Managing these *relationships* is at the heart of leadership" (Guillot 62).

In the ***Communal Domain of Leadership***, there are two building blocks: *impact* and *stewardship*.

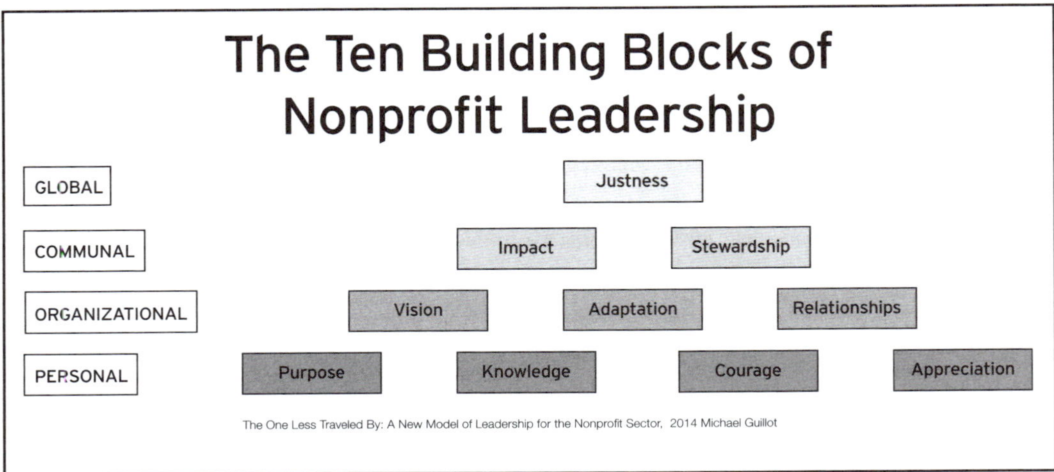

Michael states that he uses *impact* "to emphasize the importance of leadership within the community to make a difference, to produce positive effects beyond the organization" (Guillot 62). With *stewardship*, he claims that "leaders must serve as *stewards* of that trust and that benefit. '*Stewardship* is defined as the choice to preside over the orderly distribution of power. It is the willingness to be accountable for the well-being of the larger organization by operating in service to, rather than in control of, those around us. It is accountability without control or compliance'" (Guillot 63).

In the ***Global Domain***, there is one last building block at the top of the pyramid – *justness*. "*Justness* is the rightful outcome of nonprofit leadership. Authentic leaders are not motivated by compliance, but by commitment. Their sense of purpose is animated by a sense of vocation, of calling, of work that serves a mission they care deeply about and seeks to advance their community and the world. In this, the connection goes beyond local. In this, we see our common humanity and our global sharing" (Guillot 63). With such an interesting word, Michael wraps up this final building block by saying, "(*Justness*) implies that decisions are made on merit with all sides treated rightfully and neither getting more or less than warranted. A leader accepting *justness* as an overarching trait will then bring this virtue into every matter and use it as a guideline for his leadership" (Guillot 63).

It is indeed sad that Michael submitted his dissertation in September of 2014, and six months later he passed away. But, what a legacy he has left – not only with his past history of excellence as a Catholic school leader but as the author of a culture-changing philosophy on organizational leadership. Indeed, with this lesson, it really does come down to those two words – leadership and attitude.

Lesson 4: Build Community through Communication.

Many years ago, I was conducting a series of *development* workshops for Catholic schools in the Diocese of Syracuse. I remember at one of the workshops, Bishop Moynihan pulled me aside and asked an intriguing question. He said, "Frank, in working with other Catholic schools and parishes, what do you feel is the biggest challenge we face here at the close of the century?"

My response was two-fold as I said, "Bishop, I believe there are two main challenges. The first is seeking to meaningfully engage more people into the life of our schools and parishes; and secondly, making sure we have effective communication."

In many of the Catholic school planning efforts with which we have been involved, it seems that leaders want to address many of the following areas with creative and proven strategies:

- Advancing the Catholic identity
- Addressing the enrollment challenges
- Handling the costs of running a Catholic school
- Attracting and sustaining outstanding leaders for our schools
- Managing the changing demographics
- Maintaining an outstanding academic/technology curriculum
- Further establishing a vibrant student activities program
- Addressing the facility needs
- Creating a "customer service" and "people engagement" culture
- Making sure that Catholic schools tell their story in an effective and appealing way

With all of this, we come to the realization that a major key to moving forward is the word *communication*. These are questions and statements we hear all the time:

- "Does the right hand know what the left hand is doing here?"
- "When did they decide to do that?"
- "The parish and the school are just simply not on the same page."
- "No one really knows what other groups are doing around here."
- "Why do they always send so much direct mail? So many people simply do not read that stuff anymore."
- "When is anyone ever going to talk face to face with someone so we can understand what is going on?"
- "I know they say they have a plan and a vision for the future, but I sure have not seen or heard anything."

Talk with most Catholic leaders today, and they will say that communication is one of the most important areas they need to address. Yet, when push comes to shove, many Catholic schools rely on communication vehicles that are basic yet not the most effective. Communication instruments like direct mail, e-mail, text messages, web sites, messages sent home with students, etc. can be somewhat effective, but let's further explore.

Years ago, as we often tell the story, we were asked to conduct a survey among three parishes with elementary schools that were geographically very close to each other. The parish/school leaders wanted to find out a bunch of things, but one of the questions had to do with communication. Here was the question, which was specifically applicable to those parishes and schools:

Please rank in order of effectiveness ("1" being the least effective and "5" being the most effective) the following communication vehicles:

_____ Personal letter from the pastor/principal/teacher with a personal note in the margin

_____ Fellow parishioner/school leader speaking from the pulpit

_____ Pastor/principal speaking from the pulpit

_____ Parish bulletin

_____ E-mail to parishioners/parents

_____ Flyers posted outside of church and/or school

Based upon approximately 1,000 surveys that were returned, here is how the parents and parishioners voted, ranked from most effective to least effective:

1: Personal letter from the pastor/principal/teacher (most effective)

2: Fellow parishioner/school leader speaking from the pulpit

3: Pastor/principal speaking from the pulpit

4: E-mail to parishioners/parents

5: Flyers posted outside of church and/or school

6: Parish bulletin (least effective)

Interesting, indeed. Now, we are not saying that the above is right or wrong; we are only pointing out that in these three parishes and schools the parishioners and parents voted and that was the priority order.

To drive our point home, the parish bulletin came in last. And yet, when we ask parish leaders all over the country what is the main vehicle for communication, 95% will usually say, "The parish bulletin." To carry this even further, in most parishes the only people who get the parish bulletin are those who come to celebrate liturgy on the weekends; most parishes do not mail the bulletin home. And, parish leaders say, "I got you covered! We post it on our website!" And, our response is always, "Do you really think that those people who do not come to Mass on the weekends are going to rush to your website to read the bulletin?"

Because of time, money and personnel, many Catholic schools and parishes are not able to communicate effectively to all key constituents. Many Catholic leaders believe that bulletins, announcements, website postings, emails, direct mail, flyers and posters, recorded messages, newsletters, and even school apps for smart phones are going to carry the messages that will be understood, acted upon, and move people to action. We find that the above vehicles are good for three things:

- They announce.
- They position.
- They reinforce.

With website postings, folks have to know how to get to your website and furthermore, it has to be interesting enough to drive them to action. With e-mails, they have to know who is sending it, and furthermore, they have to want to open it. With direct mail, people on your database have to wade through all the other pieces they receive in their mailbox. With flyers and posters, people have to be present physically to read them. With recorded messages, they have to make sure they check the machine and the message has to be timely, based upon when they check it. With school apps for smartphones, the recipients still have to open up that application on a regular basis. And, with newsletters, there has to be information (both visually and in the written word) that is interesting and relevant to their situation.

All Catholic schools are challenged to communicate effectively. That is why we always recommend that Catholic schools actively communicate with every stakeholder at least seven times per year, and two of those times should be "eyeball to eyeball." So many of the suggested communication vehicles listed above are passive and indirect. They require the stakeholders (parents, prospective families, new families, alumni, key donors, students, past parents, grandparents, friends, etc.) to take an active role in getting the information. In other words, the school is not going out to the stakeholders. And, we believe that if we are going to communicate our vision, mission, values, goals and WOW, we need to be pro-active. We need to engage; we need to build community; we need to drive to action; we need to do everything possible to interact and build long-lasting relationships. And, quite simply, that usually does not happen when we churn out information that requires the recipient of that information to make a move to receive it.

It all goes back to people. Over and over again, even though it takes time, even though it requires more personnel, and even though it may require more resources, we are going to become much more effective when we can use all of the above vehicles to announce, position and reinforce, and then use "eyeball to eyeball" work to move to action and build relationships. It is this second part of the communication equation that is missing.

In our experiences in working with Catholic schools, here is what we have found and measured through the years. Using direct mail, e-mail, text messaging, and web-site postings to build relationships, most Catholic leaders will be effective 5% - 8% of the time (hence the personal letter). Over the phone, leaders can be effective 15% - 18% of the time (hence the value of phone outreach with dialogue). But, when we want to make sure that the message is getting across, and we are actively seeking to engage someone, then we need to move to "eyeball to eyeball." One on one meetings, small group discussions, and even large group meetings can be effective as much as 45% - 55% of the time.

For example, if we build our enrollment management efforts totally around direct mail, open houses, and visits to feeder sources, then we are not going to be as effective as if we interact with prospective families by getting them on campus for activities, games and events. We need to have our parents and students call and engage the prospective parent and/or student in a conversation. Or, we need to invite prospective families onto our campus to participate in a planning process or offer educational opportunities about student life in high school or in elementary school. *People give to people.* They give their time; they give their energy; they give their wisdom; they give their children to a Catholic school where they can trust those who are the leaders. They give their families to a parish where they believe they can grow spiritually and be part of that faith community.

There are so many ways to create "eyeball to eyeball" communication, but it takes a commitment to, and an understanding of, the value. Here are some very effective ways to interact and connect:

- Interviews
- Breakfast/luncheon/dinner meetings
- Visits in the home
- Planning sessions
- Input sessions
- Class by class parent meetings
- Alumni reunions
- Town Hall Meetings/Convocations
- Informal cup of coffee meetings at your "shop"
- New parent visits
- Neighborhood meetings
- Pastor, principal, president cabinet meetings twice per year

The list goes on and on. If we want to move people to action and convince them of something, then we need to do it "eyeball to eyeball." Are we saying that "eyeball to eyeball" is the only way and everything else is ineffective? No. What we are saying is that we need a good mix of all of the communication vehicles. And, that becomes our challenge: building the foundation of our Catholic schools with a seamless, relationship-building communication system. When we do that, then we truly build community.

Lesson 5: Move from Fund-Raising to True Catholic Development.

There are many reasons why Catholic schools initiate a *development/ advancement* effort, and a lot of those reasons center around the word "money." Now, that is not altogether wrong. However, when "money" becomes the central and only focus of the *development* office and officer, then sooner or later the effort could turn into planning one fund-raiser after another. At ISPD, we strongly believe that the fund-raising part of *development* should not be the central focus. Financial resources certainly play a part in *development*, but they should not be the only reason a *development* office is opened up for business.

As we have said, *Development is the meaningful involvement of people in your mission and vision for the future.* This defines it all. Through meaningful involvement, relationships build and the bonds between people grow stronger. It is the role of the president, the principal, the pastor, the *development* officer, and school leaders to identify, inform, invite and involve people every day into the life of the school. That becomes the theme that makes the difference.

Unfortunately, many *development* efforts are born because there is a shortfall in the budget, and the first 2-3 years are spent holding one fund-raiser after another. There are candy sales and auctions and raffles and fairs and festivals and golf tournaments and Las Vegas nights and walkathons and car washes and Easter bunny rabbit sales and magazine sales and calendar sales and bingo and dinner/ dances and on and on. Once this pattern begins, it becomes hard to break, simply because the finance committee depends upon that money to balance the books.

There are two key definitions that are important in order to understand true Catholic Development:

1. **Fund-raising dollars:** This is money generated from the fund-raising events, some of the ones listed above, for example. There is a "buy and sell" mentality here. I will buy a raffle calendar and you will sell me one. I will buy a bingo card and you will sell me one or two or more. I will buy raffle tickets and you will sell me some. What is important to understand is this: What motivates me to buy those bingo cards is what I will get in return. It makes no difference if I believe in your mission, your vision, your plan or anything about your school. I simply want to have the winning card at bingo.
2. **Development dollars:** This is philanthropic giving. I expect nothing in return. I give through the joy of giving or because I want to make things better, or because I believe in a cause or a strong case. This is the Annual Fund Drive, the Capital Campaign, the planned gift, the endowment fund, the memorial gift, the charitable remainder trust, the major gift to fund the science lab or pay for a stained glass window. In order to give *development* dollars, I need to believe in the leadership, the vision, the case, and the plan for the future. I need to feel involved and engaged. I need to belong – in some kind of way.

For those schools that want to move in that direction, there is a process that we have outlined in this book that addresses how to move from fund-raising to *development*. It does not happen overnight, and it will take a lot of education, communication and understanding. However, if your school is in for the long-term, then *development* is the right road to travel and the meaningful involvement of people is the fuel that will get you there.

There are important questions that we suggest Catholic school leaders answer. They are listed here with a short explanation.

1. **Why was the *development* effort started at your school?**
   - This is the first important question to honestly answer. Who started it and why? If it was just for money, then you need to be willing to say that. There is nothing wrong with the truth.
2. **Who is responsible for the implementation of the *development* efforts?**
   - The person and/or people in charge of your *development* efforts must understand why the efforts were begun. Is this the principal, the president, the pastor, the development director, a parent committee, a core team, etc.? When this person and/or group does implement the *development* initiatives, it will be important that they understand the next question.
3. **Does the leadership understand the difference between *development* and fund-raising?**
   - It will be important to in-service and educate the leaders on the difference between *development* and fund-raising. They do need to understand what direction the *development* efforts should be taking.
4. **Does the *development* effort have to raise a certain amount of money in order to balance the budget each year?**
   - This, too, is an important question. If you must raise a certain amount of money each year from the *development* efforts, then you may be painting yourself into a corner. By that we mean that you may be forcing the *development* office to assume a fund-raising mode 100% of the time. If that is the case, then you will never be able to move into engaging people and inviting them into your efforts. Everything will be built around events and buying and selling and not around building relationships.
5. **How many fund-raisers does your school conduct? Please name them.**
   - It will be important to name the fund-raisers – small and large – that your school is involved in. List not only the ones that are sponsored by the school, but also the ones that are sponsored by the organizations, clubs, teams, departments, etc.
6. **What kind of approval process is in place for a team, group, organization, club, class, etc. to hold a fund-raiser?**
   - Oftentimes, there is no master calendar or master plan for fund-raisers, and when a group wants to do one, they simply ask the principal, and they do it. The problem with this is that if a donor is planning on giving a $1,000 gift to the Annual Fund Drive, and his daughter asks him to buy five raffle calendars at $50.00 each for the cheerleading squad, then he may purchase the calendars, and forego any philanthropic gift to the Annual Fund. In other words, he may be saying, "I already gave." There must be a limit, and there must be a process in place in order for a parish/school to get a "grip" on its many fund-raisers.

7. Does it seem that the *development* efforts move from one fund-raising event to another?

- We talk with many development directors who go from one event to another. They are so busy printing tickets, organizing a planning committee, or seeking prizes, or booking rooms, or designing programs, or juggling one or two other fund-raisers, there never is any time to do true Catholic *development*.

8. Do your parents feel as though they are being "nickeled and dimed" to death?

- You simply will not get the philanthropic gift if all you do is have your hand out seeking another two liter coke or another set of raffle tickets or another fee to assess.

9. If you have a development director would it be best to call that person "director of fund-raising activities"?

- If you are going to call your development director a development director, then please don't have that person spend the majority of his/her time conducting fund-raising events. If the person is going to do that then be honest. Call it like it is. Simply say that the person is "director of fund-raising activities". There is nothing wrong with that.

10. How important is it for your school to move from fund-raising to *development*? Please circle below.

Very Important   Important   Not very important   NA

- This is another one of those "be brutally honest" questions. If the leadership of your school simply wants to generate $100,000 per year through six key fund-raisers, then so be it.

So, if you are serious about moving into an integrated *development* process, now is the time to begin, and there are steps listed below to make that happen.

Step 1: Educate the leadership (decision makers) of your institution on the difference between *development* and fund-raising.

Step 2: Determine how important it is for the school to move more into *development* and less into fund-raising events.

Step 3: Understand the budget considerations and what is feasible to do and what is not feasible to do.

Step 4: Create a visual called "Present Fund-raising Activities/Events." *(See Lesson 14).*

Step 5: Educate and inform all key fund-raising groups on what the present visual looks like and means.

Step 6: Form a sub-committee made up of representation from key groups within the school.

Step 7: Have the sub-committee create a mission statement, philosophy and rationale for fund-raising activities at your Catholic school.

Step 8: Have the sub-committee create an application and approval process for all fund-raising activities.

Step 9: Develop a master plan for future years (school or calendar) and highlight the following: a.) Emphasis on the annual fund; b.) 2-3 key major fundraisers; c.) Small fund-raisers that do not interfere with the present donor base.

Step 10: Have the sub-committee create an integrated annual fund in order to fund three areas: a.) Operational budget; b.) Needed funds for organizations, clubs, teams; c.) new programs.

Step 11: Seek a 12% - 15% increase in donors and a 90% -- 95% retention rate in donors each year in the Annual Appeal.

Step 12: Solidify the annual *development* revenue budget around a strong integrated annual fund and 2-3 school sponsored fund-raisers (i.e. auction, golf tourney, etc.).

Step 13: Once solidified, initiate an organized major gift process focusing on developing 50 -- 100 portfolios the first year.

Step 14: Create an orientation process for parents and alumni (before your graduates leave you) so they understand that your *development* revenue will come from those items listed in # 12 and # 13.

Step 15: Educate and inform all groups each year so that they understand that *development* $$$ are a lot more important than fund-raising $$$.

Pivotal

Lesson 6: Believe in and Promote the Value of a "Customer Service" Culture in Your Catholic School.

As we have written and spoken about "customer service" in Catholic schools, we find that those two words can be a turn-off for some Catholic leaders. Not to be taken literally, when we talk about "customer service," we really are talking about people serving one another. In other words, in a Catholic school, everyone is a "customer" of each other. "Customer service" can be found and defined in many ways:

- It is the way a "customer" is treated when she calls the school office and needs information.
- It is the way a prospective family is treated when they come to the school for a tour.
- It is the way students are treated in the classroom.
- It is the way teachers are treated when it comes time for contract renewal.
- It is the way people are affirmed and commended on a regular and consistent basis.
- It is the way new families are welcomed in their first year.
- It is the way volunteers are appreciated.
- It is the way alums are invited back to the school.
- It is the way parents are communicated with in regards to tuition and fees.
- It is the way an athlete is treated on the football field by his coaches.
- It is the way a school develops a relationship with a family.
- It is a shift in the way many Catholic schools need to operate – not to be in opposition to parents, but to be in collaboration and coordination with them.
- "Customer service" is everyone serving each other.

Why is this kind of culture so important today? In order to fully understand that, let's go back 50 years.

1967 was my first year of teaching; I was able to land a teaching position at my alma mater – De La Salle High School in New Orleans. Back then, there were waiting lists for every class. I was one of 8-10 lay teachers who taught there, and the rest were La Sallian Christian Brothers. "Technology" was an opaque projector, a hand cranked ditto machine with purple ink, and a slide strip projector that I used to teach the eight parts of speech. In my first year of teaching, my salary was $4,800, and I know you won't believe this now, but I could not believe they would pay me that much to do something that I truly loved. In addition, I taught five sophomore English classes and one 8th grade geography class. Each class had approximately 35-40 students in it. Back then, the budget was balanced with tuition, subsidies, and a couple of good fund-raisers (like a fair or a festival).

Fast forward to 2016. We live in a totally different world. Today, there is competition from everywhere – for students, for teachers, for administrators, and more. Notice just some of the changes:

- 99% of the faculty are lay women and men.
- Technology costs have soared.
- Academic advances are mind-boggling.
- Girls' athletics has become just as important as boys' athletics.
- Public relations and marketing have become key to future success, and because of that, the principal's role has drastically changed.
- President-principal models have thrived in many areas.
- Faculty and staff have been invited to step forward beyond their field(s) of certification and into the world of public relations and marketing.
- *Development/advancement* offices have become the norm in both high schools and elementary schools.
- Long-range planning is a must-do.
- Enrollment management is the new language.
- "Branding" your image is now crucial to name recognition.
- 7 and 8 figure endowments are now important to long-range success.
- Facilities must keep up with the quality of the curriculum.
- Alums, parents, past parents, community, friends, and others are now important in order to remain viable in the marketplace.
- 'Development" must mean more than selling candy and putting on B-I-N-G-O.
- Marketing must be more than inviting your present parents to an open house.

In our work with Catholic schools across the nation, we see seven major challenge areas that keep many Catholic school leaders awake at night. They are:

- Revenue and resources
- Enrollment
- Attracting and retaining quality personnel
- Leadership
- Parish and school collaboration (where applicable)
- Vision, mission, and plans for the future
- Facility needs and demands

Understanding and integrating a "customer service" culture goes a long way in addressing the challenges that face our Catholic schools. We believe that in order to solve these challenges, it is imperative that we shift the culture of our Catholic schools into being more "customer" oriented. In today's economy, people want value and choices; they want to be treated equally and fairly; they want quality, and they want to feel as though they belong to a community that is making a difference – one that is welcoming, inviting and engaging.

Today, many people who are involved or could be involved in our Catholic schools are looking for benefits – what will best serve them and their family? Here is a question we often ask, so please agree or disagree. *A Catholic school will only attract the number of resources (financial, people, community, connections, etc.) that it deserves to attract. And, what it deserves to attract will be in direct relationship to the quality of its leadership, programs, processes, and "customer service" attitude.*

Because we believe that "customer service" is so important, here is one final question we always ask when working with Catholic school leaders, volunteers, and donors: "Here at (name of school) do you feel you belong?" Please remember again: Belonging leads to believing, and in a "customer service" culture, everyone should have the opportunity to belong – every day.

Customers are who you serve and who serve you.

Lesson 7: Build Relationships with Your School Families.

Back in the 1960's when I was a young teenager, I remember that one of the highlights of my family's year was when "Father Bob" would come for his annual visit to our home. This was a two hour affair with dinner, conversation, and fellowship. After the meal, I remember my brother and I were told to "go outside and play" or, basically, disappear for a while so "Father Bob" and my mom and dad could continue talking. You see, I was raised in the Episcopal Church, and this was simply part of being a family in that parish. Those visits continued for many years, even with pastor changes, and the relationships that were established, and the sense of stewardship that was fostered, grew stronger and stronger. In 1975, I went through the RCIA program at Immaculate Conception Church in the Archdiocese of New Orleans and converted to the Roman Catholic faith. Unlike my Episcopal journey, there were no visits to my Catholic family.

Today Catholic parishes and schools are faced with challenges that are quite daunting. Every week, as we consult and teach throughout the country, we see these challenges knocking many Catholic institutions back on their heels, and even some of them out of the total picture. We all know what they are:

- Lack of parishioner involvement;
- Decreasing enrollment in Catholic schools;
- Costs of running Catholic schools;
- Leadership in our parishes and schools;
- Changing demographics;
- Facility needs of our parishes and schools;
- Lack of a "customer service" and "people engagement" culture;
- Boss management vs. team management;
- Wanting dynamic change but doing the same things over and over again.

This is not to say that there are not Catholic schools who are moving forward in a visionary and dynamic manner. There are many solutions that are being tried. Some of them work, and some of them do not work. President-principal structures, new enrollment management strategies, direct mail campaigns, strategic planning efforts, more personnel in the *advancement/development* office, better *stewardship* processes, more fund-raising events, mergers, customer service training, new board restructuring, capital campaigns, new governance and operational models, business community relationships/partnerships – the list goes on and on. And, interestingly, with the right leadership and direction, many of the above do work.

Rule of Insanity - always doing things the same way = Insanity

We would like to take this a step further and address a topic that we have talked about for the past 10+ years. It is a topic that usually meets with two responses and then is quickly dismissed. Those two responses are:

- "Interesting."
- "Yeah, right. You must be out of your mind!"

Here is our belief: *In order for Catholic schools to prevail and meet the daunting challenges we are facing, we must figure out the ways, means and processes for school leaders to meet with every family one-on-one at least once per year for a lengthy conversation in their home or on the school site – "eyeball to eyeball."* Interesting! Yeah, right!

We understand the cost. We understand the logistics. We understand the time commitment, and we understand the personnel factor. However, if we really believe that *people engagement* and *meaningful involvement* and *fostering true stewardship* are important beliefs in Catholic *development*, then we need to make this happen.

Let us say that your school – over the next year – was able to recruit and train 5-10 teams with two people on each team. Sample combinations:

- Principal and faculty/staff member
- Two board members
- Two faculty/staff members
- Two parent leaders
- Two alum leaders
- Faculty member and parent leader

Let us look at the conversation topics and the advantages of building the relationships with each and every school family:

- What the school teams can discuss and share with a school family:
    - Vision and plans for the future of the school;
    - Overall progress of the children as students in the school;
    - Changes in the school and how they will impact that family;
    - How the school operates;
    - Ways of engagement and involvement that family members would enjoy;
    - Discussion of the family's gifts of prayer and involvement;

- Discussion of the family's financial commitment to the Catholic school:
    - Tuition and fees
    - In-kind giving
    - Annual fund
    - Fund-raisers
    - Ways the family can generate financial resources for the school
- After discussing the above, the school team (of two) need to sit back and ask this question: *Mr. and Mrs. Johnson (or Ms. Johnson or Mr. Wilson or whatever), what we would like you to do is share with us how (name of school) can better serve you and how we can continue to build a strong relationship with your family that will last a lifetime. What are your needs? How can we help you meet those needs? What gifts would you enjoy sharing with the school? How can we help each of your children as students in our school?*

Now before we hit the panic button on this one, let's set some guidelines and state some basic tenets.

- We are not saying that this needs to be put in place next month. We are inviting you to begin serious discussions with your school leaders about how this would be possible and why this would be so valuable.
- As a Catholic school, you may begin to look at sitting down between May and August with every new family that will attend your school in the next school year. Can you imagine the PR and the response out in the community as your new families talk about this one-on-one experience with other families? How their Catholic school actually takes the time to sit down and personally discuss their situation? How their Catholic school is all about building relationships and really engaging people?
- In order to be perfectly clear: the goal here is to visit with EVERY family in your school (elementary school, high school, regional school, etc.) once per year and engage in a meaningful conversation.
- The advantages are overwhelming. Every new family in your school would know from the "get-go" that this is the way you build your faith community – one by one. This would become the new norm. This would be the way that school leaders could track progress from year to year. Naturally, forms will have to be created; files will have to be kept, and the two most important components of all of this are RESPONSE and CONFIDENTIALITY. The ability to respond to the needs of each family will mean the difference between success or failure.
- This is setting up the Catholic high school, elementary school, Pre-K -- 12 school operation with a totally new modus operandi. It is exciting, and the contacts, the resources, the relationships, and the connections have the potential to be unbelievable.

Before you begin to quickly dismiss, let's go back to the challenges and look at how this *personal relationship building campaign* can address the very concerns that keep Catholic leaders awake at night.

- Decreasing enrollment in Catholic schools;

This could be discussed with invitations for families to make referrals and the personal visit certainly would be building a very strong retention action.

- Costs of running Catholic schools;
  - This could finally be explained in full -- how tuition does NOT cover the cost of educating a child in a Catholic school.
- Leadership in our Catholic schools;
  - This could un-surface many potential volunteer leaders for the school.
- Changing demographics;
  - The visiting team could learn many things about the area, the neighborhood and the families living in that area.
- Facility needs of our schools;
  - The case for support plus the identification of facilities needs could all be part of this conversation.
- Lack of a "customer service" and "people engagement" culture;
  - With the family visits, this is exactly what you would be doing – serving the customer and engaging the family.
- Boss management vs. team management;

It would be easily seen that the Catholic institution's management style is collaborative and inviting.

- Wanting dynamic change but doing the same things over and over again.
  - This is major change.

So, what do we have to do to convince Catholic leaders to open up the discussions on this topic? This will vastly change the way we operate as Catholic institutions. This outreach can be integrated into the culture of your Catholic school, and ten years from now we will not be saying, "How do we keep the doors open?" but, "Can you believe how strong a faith community we have now that we have opened wide the doors to Christ?"

Lesson 8: Promote the Value of Faculty/Staff and Board Involvement in Development.

Two of the main questions we always ask when we work with the *development/advancement* efforts of a Catholic school are: 1. Does your faculty/staff understand what you do in *development* and visa-versa? 2. How much is the board involved in the *development* efforts here at the school? Many times the answers are "No" and "Very little."

Although surprising to many, in our workshops we have always said that *the most important group of people to a Catholic school development effort is the faculty/staff.* Why? They live the mission of the school each and every day. And, happy, motivated and positive faculty and staff members lead to happy, motivated and positive students which leads to happy, motivated and positive parents which leads to wonderful public relations and image out in the community.

An important lesson we have learned through the years is to make sure that those people working in *development* do everything possible to get to know the faculty and staff of the school. It is also important that the faculty and staff learn what Catholic school *development* is all about and how important the *development* efforts are to the present state and the future of the school. We have gone so far as to recommend that the development officers schedule lunches or cup of coffee meetings with every faculty/staff member throughout the year. They need to know what is going on with the *development* efforts, and the development officers need to understand what is going on in the classrooms and other areas of the school. Faculty/staff members make excellent *core team* members; they can work with a strategic planning process; they can chair the leadership division of the annual fund; they can serve as ambassadors at open house; they can serve on the marketing or enrollment management committees; they can help with the alumni – especially if they are alums. There are so many opportunities for faculty/staff members to become involved. The key will be to break out of old ways of thinking and reach out and get to know the people who teach the students and answer the phones and serve in the cafeteria.

Another action step that many Catholic schools take is to create a one page *development update* bulletin that could come out on a monthly basis. It can be word-processed and e-mailed to administration, faculty/staff, parent leaders, alumni leaders, student council members, and board members. This communication piece lets school leaders read what is going on in *development* on a monthly basis. Once the *development update* is in place, you should never hear the question, "When did they decide to do that?" It is so important to keep the faculty/staff informed and involved. Development is the key to their future.

There are some Catholic schools that do an excellent job of keeping their boards involved and engaged in *development* efforts, and there are others where the board members just sit in judgment of how much money is being raised. Dr. Regina Haney (formerly with NCEA) and I have presented many webinars about a Catholic school board's role in *development.* We usually refer to five major points in our presentations:

1. As a board member, seek to understand that Catholic school *development* is not just about raising money.

2. Work with the school's administration, the faculty/staff, and the *development* personnel to build a culture of belonging.
3. Roll up your sleeves and work with the *development* efforts of the school.
   - Serve on the *development core team.*
   - Be a chairperson and a leader in the annual fund.
   - Work with the school's strategic planning process.
   - Constantly identify people who can make a difference for the school.
   - Get to know the personnel in *development* and work with them to advance the school.
4. Make sure that the school has a vision and a long-range plan for the future.
5. Be a "giver" and a "getter."
   - Be willing to "give" your own resources to the school.
   - Be willing to "get" others to give their resources to the school.

Although a short one, Lesson 8 is important. The wonderful thing about Catholic school *development* – when implemented correctly – is that it is always inclusive and never exclusive. We strongly recommend that those in charge of the school's *development* make every effort to consistently invite and involve the faculty/staff and the board. For, as we said, the future advancement and vitality of the school is in the interest of everyone – especially those two groups of people.

SECTION C: PROCESSES AND STRUCTURES TO ADVANCE CATHOLIC SCHOOLS

Lesson 9: Emphasize the Value of the Development Core Team.

In the mid-'90's, I was presenting a two-day workshop on Catholic school *development* in the Diocese of San Jose. At the end of the first day, I was approached by a pastor and a principal from a parochial school, and here is what they said. "Frank, we are really enjoying this workshop – excellent information. However, as we listen and as we discuss, it sounds like all of this is giving more work to the principal and the pastor of a Catholic school. Who is going to do all of this – especially if we do not have a full time development director or no director at all?"

What an excellent question! At the time, I did not have a detailed answer. I talked about delegation and prioritization, and what was important to do first, but I never gave them an answer that I thought was substantial. After that workshop, I came back to the office, and I can remember discussing the question at our next staff meeting. And so, over the next six months or so, we developed this *core team* concept. I am proud to say that we have taught and consulted on this topic for many years, and we have seen hundreds of *core teams* be created and accomplish great things. In this lesson, let me elaborate on what a *development core team* is all about.

The *core team* that works with the *development* efforts of a Catholic school is a group of 15+ dedicated and committed people who create, implement and sustain the *development* processes. The *core team* works hand-in-hand with the *development* office. The initial thrust is toward the following:

- Understanding the scope of Catholic school *development*;
- Introducing *development* to the school community;
- Identifying the *development* challenges the school faces;
- Helping solve those challenges by creating the *strategic plan for development*;
- Rolling up their sleeves and implementing the strategic initiatives coming out of the *strategic plan*.

Qualities and Selection

1. The people who serve on the *core team* usually come from the "first ripple."
2. They need to be positive, mission-driven individuals who strongly believe in the school and where it is going.
3. They should be able to work in a team setting, and be team players.

4. At least one-half of the members should be able to speak well in front of a small or large group of people, especially as this applies to teaching others what Catholic school *development* is all about and what the *development* efforts are in their Catholic school.
5. Besides the administration, representation could come from:
   - School councils/boards
   - Faculty/staff
   - Parent leaders
   - Alumni leaders
   - Key donor(s) -- actual or potential
6. The administration should select the people to serve on the *core team*, and the principal needs to personally invite these people -- by phone or in person.
7. After the initial meeting, it may be necessary to add or amend the original list in order to get good representation.
8. It will be important to have the names, addresses, phone numbers, fax numbers, and e-mail addresses of the members of this team, so they can stay informed every step of the way.

Roles and Responsibilities

1. To serve as the "steering wheel" to the *development* process:
   - Educate – 10%
   - Facilitate – 10%
   - Implement – 80%
2. To provide background information and any historical perspective that may be needed as they move through the *development* processes;
3. To identify people in the school who will be asked to get involved in this *development* effort:
   - 60% new
   - 40% already involved
4. To help invite these people to become involved
   - Input sessions
   - Planning teams
   - Financial leaders
5. To serve as spokespersons for the *development* efforts in case anyone in the school wishes to find out more about them;
6. To share any concern or issue that needs to be discussed before it can reach the problem stage out in the parish/school community;

7. To honor the confidentiality of the information that is discussed in this *core team* -- especially as it concerns other individual members of the school community;
8. To serve in leadership positions when asked to do so -- for example, to help facilitate input sessions or small group meetings or serve as the chair of the annual fund or help with the school's open house;
9. To offer news and bulletin information that would be pertinent to an internal *development Update* that should be in circulation -- which will originate from the *core team*;
10. To always remain positive and vision-driven.

Keys to a Successful Development Core Team

1. Committed -- not just interested
2. Members are prompt and on time for meetings.
3. Meetings begin on time and end on time.
4. There is an agenda for each meeting.
5. There is a report from each meeting with the results shared with team members before the next meeting.
6. Team members respect each other's opinions -- although they may not always agree on everything.
7. The *core team* is geared toward four major areas:
    - Helping guide and facilitate the *development* processes
    - Offering key suggestions for success
    - Helping implement key strategies
    - Continuing education
8. All ideas are discussed out in the open, and conversations do not continue into the "parking lot" with hidden agendas. The *core team* must be solid and members must trust one another.
9. The mission of the *core team* must be clear to all.

What is important to remember is that the *core team* can work with any situation:

- *Development* effort with no *development* personnel;
- One part-time or full-time development officer;
- Multi-person office.

In many cases, the development officer in a Catholic school is the "plate spinner in the circus." And, oftentimes, some of those plates stop spinning because there is just too much to do and too little time to do it. The *development core team* is an answer that deserves attention and implementation.

Lesson 10: Seek Input from Your Constituents on a Consistent Basis.

Father Jim Manning, president of Archbishop Alter High School in Dayton, Ohio, and the person who serves as the spiritual advisor for ISPD, has long been a believer in the meaningful involvement of people. Through the years, we have had many conversations about inviting people, and I have heard Father Jim often say, "It is so important to 'pipeline' to your people."

There are many ways that Catholic schools seek input, and we wish there were more schools that would reach out and invite parents, students, alums, faculty/staff, prospective families, potential donors, businesses, and others to offer their perspectives and opinions. Is this risky? Will you hear the good, the bad and the ugly? Yes. However, that is also operating from a position of strength. How can a Catholic school know how it is doing in the "marketplace" if it does not ask?

Through the years we have seen and used many different vehicles to seek input; however, after all of this time, we have come to settle on two main processes that we would like to recommend: 1. Input Sessions and 2. The Ultimate Question. Let us explain.

Input Sessions

We define an input session as a meeting of 10 – 20 people who are <u>randomly</u> invited to attend a 50-55 minute session and focus on two or three specific topics for discussion. The input session is facilitated; there is a clear agenda, and the session does not last longer than 50-55 minutes.

As part of the 7 "I" processes of *development*, the input session fits into the *invite* stage. This is an excellent way to invite people and get them interested in what is going on in your school. In the beginning of your relationship with them -- whether they are a parent, alum, or donor -- it is important for you to get to know them and visa-versa. Input sessions provide that introduction and invitation.

When done correctly, we find them to be very successful for the following reasons:

- People are personally invited.
- The person inviting them is the principal or the president.
- Invitees are given a choice of times and dates.
- People really enjoy giving their opinions.
- A personal phone call from the *core team* is the follow-up.
- They know they are not being asked to serve on a committee that meets forever.
- They know they are being asked to attend a session that only lasts for one hour at the most.
- There is an established agenda.

Through the years, we have found that input sessions can allow you to identify many of the future leaders of your school community. It is an excellent way to begin the relationship. Usually there are 3-4 questions that are asked:

1. What impresses you about the school?
2. What are those areas of the school that you would like to see improved?
3. As you look to the future, what would you like to see in the next 1-3-5 years?

The process we have recommended goes like this:

1. Randomly select the people you wish to invite from a list that is provided. Please keep in mind that approximately 30% of the people invited will attend -- if conducted properly. Obviously, depending on the audience, you will have greater attendance from different groups. Usually the reason the percentage of people who attend is not higher than 30% is that you are using a random selection.
2. Plan to conduct either 2 or 3 nights of input sessions with 3 sessions per night.
   - 6:00 PM
   - 7:00 PM
   - 8:00 PM
3. You want to invite three times more people than you expect. If you get more, that is great.
4. With a list of 540 names, and two nights of input sessions (six sessions) scheduled, for example, you need to invite 200 people or every third name on the list.
5. Letters are mailed out that are personally addressed.
6. Within one week, there is the follow-up phone call from a credible person at the school.
7. When people arrive, greeters (possibly students) show them where to park and show them where to go for the session.
8. You should have the following:
   - Name tags
   - Refreshments
   - The principal and/or *core team* personally thanking people for coming
   - Signs up pointing the way
9. At five minutes to the hour, people are invited into the room.
10. The input session is conducted.
11. As people leave, *core team* members thank them and invite them for a cup of coffee and some cookies.
12. Within 2-3 weeks of the input session, there is an input session report that is mailed to all people who attended listing the highlights. This report summarizes all of the sessions.
13. A thank you letter is sent with the report or before it.

There are established procedures and guidelines that we see working, and those are:

1. The room should be arranged in a circle or semi-circle so people can see each other.
2. The facilitator needs to be at the focal point of the room. This could be a *core team* member.
3. There should be a scribe that the school appoints.
4. The principal can say the opening prayer and then thank people for attending. After that introduction, the principal should leave.
5. The input session is handed over to the facilitator.
6. The facilitator follows this process:
    - Introduces himself/herself
    - Has each person introduce himself/herself and state relationship with the school
    - Goes over the guidelines
    - Introduces the first question and opens up the discussion
    - Keeps track of time every step of the way
    - At 10 minutes to the hour, the facilitator wraps up the session and has people walking out by 5 minutes to the hour.
7. Written guidelines should be distributed at the beginning of the session.
    - We would like to hear from everyone.
    - Everyone is on equal ground.
    - This is not a gripe session.
    - We are not here to discuss personalities.
    - We are not here to argue.
    - We will be finished in 50-55 minutes.
    - You will receive a written report within 2-4 weeks.
8. The facilitator and the scribe should pay close attention to those people that raise key issues and seem to want to get more involved in the future. The scribe should write down those names. That is why "big" name tags are essential.

The written report is done after all the sessions and usually follows this outline:

- Purpose of the Input Sessions
- Times and places
- Questions asked
- Key issues raised
- Major "threads" that could be woven throughout all the sessions
- Future focus

Input sessions are a wonderful way to engage people who are not involved, simply because the people who are selected are randomly chosen. We find that people will attend these sessions because of five reasons:

1. The invitation is personalized.
2. They know the questions beforehand because they have been mentioned in the invite letter.
3. They can have their choice of dates and times.
4. The input session only lasts for one hour.
5. Most people like to give their opinions.

The Ultimate Question

The Ultimate Question is not a new book on theology. The book's author is Fred Reichheld. Harvard Business Press published the book in 2006. It has a broad application to just about any organization including Catholic schools. One of the main outcomes of this survey is getting the school's Net Promoter Score, or NPS. This is based on the fundamental perspective that every Catholic school's "customers" (parents, students, staff, alumni, prospective parents, etc.) can be divided into three categories: **Promoters**, **Passives** and **Detractors**.

By asking one simple question – How likely is it that you would recommend (your Catholic school) to a friend or colleague? – you can track these groups and get a clear measure of your school's performance through your customer's eyes. Customers respond on a 0-to-10 point scale and are categorized as follows:

- **Promoters** (score 9-10) are loyal enthusiasts who will keep "buying" and refer others, fueling growth.
- **Passives** (score 7-8) are satisfied but unenthusiastic customers who are vulnerable to competitive offerings.
- **Detractors** (score 0-6) are unhappy customers who can damage your brand and impede growth through negative word-of-mouth.

To calculate your school's NPS, you would take the percentage of customers who are Promoters and subtract the percentage who are Detractors.

- NPS = % of Promoters (9s and 10s) - % of Detractors (0 through 6)
- NOTE: Passives are not counted into the formula.

There is also a Part B to the question. After circling a number 1 thru 10, the person filling in the survey is then asked to respond to Part B. "If you did not give us a score of 10, please explain what we need to do and/or address so that the next time you take this survey, the score you give us will either be a 10 or close to it." Obviously, this provides some excellent qualitative data that can then be categorized and used in numerous ways.

We recommend that a Catholic school should ask *The Ultimate Question* at least once a year. In our work with Catholic schools, we find that the following NPS percentages represent what is acceptable and what is not.

- Outstanding: Above 65%
- Average: 50% - 64%
- Below Average: 35% - 49%
- Dismal: Below 34%

As we said, in building your *development* efforts around the 7 "I"s (*identify, inform, invite, involve, implement, invest*, and *improve*) and consistently seeking input from your constituents, plugs into the most important "I" of them all: *invite*. Through input sessions and The Ultimate Question survey, Catholic schools can personally invite people to belong.

Lesson 11: Assess Your Development Efforts.

It is important that Catholic schools assess their *development* efforts at the end of each school year – in some kind of comprehensive manner. There are many ways for Catholic schools to assess:

- Using an outside evaluation/assessment where a company/firm would come in and assess from an objective point of view;
- Having the governance/advisory board or council or committee assess what is going well and what needs to be improved;
- Having the principal and/or president assess the Catholic school *development* efforts;
- With the use of a *development core team*, having this group of people offer their assessment of what is working well and what is not;
- Bringing together a core group of people (possibly the principal, board chair, development officer, assistant principal, etc.) and having them assess the efforts.

In using any one or more of the above, there are different ways to approach the assessment:

- Open discussion of what went well and what can be improved;
- Interviews with the development officer(s);
- Group discussion using the SWOT formula:
    - Present strengths
    - Present weaknesses
    - Future opportunities
    - Future threats
- Use of some assessment tool.

In the Addendum of this book there is an assessment exercise that many schools have used, and they find it quite helpful in affirming what is going well and zeroing in on what needs to be improved. (***See ISPD Assessment Exercise***). Let's look further into this lesson and the use of this assessment tool.

In using the assessment exercise that is in the Addendum of this book, we are assuming the following:

- You have a group of people who are working on your development efforts – paid and/or unpaid.
- Your leaders have a basic understanding of what Catholic school *development* is and what it is not.
- Your assessment efforts will be positioned from the standpoint of continuous improvement.
- Many schools have one person offices as well as multiple person offices.
- Out of the 30 areas in the assessment, there will be those that some schools do not have in place.
- You are planning on using this assessment exercise as a way to learn and grow.

ISPD Assessment Exercise for Catholic School Development Efforts

This assessment is built around the following guidelines:

- There are 30 areas to assess.
- Each statement should be scored with a 0, 1, 2, 3, or NA.
    - 0: False or no accomplishment
    - 1: Somewhat true/somewhat false – minimal accomplishment
    - 2: True: average accomplishment – met basic expectations
    - 3: Very true – outstanding accomplishment
    - NA: Not Applicable
- There is room for a possible score for each statement and a total score for each area.
- There is a comment section built in.
- This assessment should be done individually first and then meet together as a group to come up with a group answer.
- We encourage using the group scores to set up goals and priorities for the next year.
- Each school should come out of the evaluation process with the following results:
    - Affirmation of what you are doing well
    - Areas of improvement and what to do
    - Areas that need addressing for the first time
    - Goals and priorities
    - Your *advancement* "game plan"

Assessment Exercise

Assessment Area 1: Team Dynamics

______Those working in Catholic *development* meet on a regular basis and are able to end this year with a good sense of accomplishment.

______There is a sense of "team" behind the Catholic school *development* efforts this year.

______Meetings are organized, regular, well facilitated and agendas drive the discussion.

______The team is clear on its mission, goals and priorities for the year.

______The principal/pastor/president serves the team well as a mentor, resource, and point person when needed.

______The person in charge of *development* serves the team well as an organizer, motivator and driver of the *development* processes.

Possible Score: 18

Total Score: _____

Comments:____

Assessment Area 2: Day to Day Operations

_____With those working in Catholic *development*, job descriptions are clear and there is little confusion as to who does what.

_____Privacy and confidentiality are respected by all people working with the Catholic *development* efforts.

_____Those working in Catholic *development* have the equipment, materials, and supplies that are needed to operate a successful effort.

_____Weekly/monthly/annual goals are set, discussed and celebrated.

_____There is adequate physical space for the *development* effort.

_____There are regularly scheduled meetings to discuss the challenges and action plans.

Possible Score: 18

Total Score: _____

Comments:____

Assessment Area 3: Role of the Pastor, Principal, President

_____There are regularly scheduled meetings with the people in charge of the Catholic school *development* efforts.

_____The pastor, principal and/or president play an active role in the implementation and success of the Catholic *development* efforts.

_____The pastor, principal and/or president see *development* as an on-going process of developing the many resources of the school.

_____The pastor, principal and/or president are the public voice and face of the *development* effort.

_____The pastor, principal and/or president play an active role in personally inviting people to join the *development* effort.

Possible Score: 15

Total Score: _____

Comments:____

Assessment Area 4: The Core Team

_____There is a *core team* (15-18) that continues to serve as a vital component to the Catholic *development* efforts.

_____Members of the *core team* are committed, engaged, and attend meetings on a regular basis.

_____The *core team* members represent many different groups, (parents, alums, faculty/staff, past parents, etc.) of the school.

_____The *core team* members see themselves as "roll up your sleeve" workers and not "back seat drivers."

_____The *core team* members are helping to implement the priorities of the *development* action plan.

_____The *core team* members understand Catholic *development* and have been educated on the value of "people fuel."

Possible Score: 18

Total Score: _____

Comments:____

Assessment Area 5: Internal Communication and Rapport

_____Those working in Catholic school *development* are able to communicate well with the faculty/staff about the team's activities.

_____The team is able to communicate with parish (if applicable) and school leaders (parish council, ministry leaders, advisory councils and boards) about the team's activities.

_____The team communicates well with the students.

_____The team communicates well with the alumni.

_____The team communicates well with parishioners (if applicable).

_____The team communicates well with parents.

_____The team has the opportunity to do some education about Catholic school *development* with the above groups.

Possible Score: 21

Total Score: _____

Comments:____

Assessment Area 6: The Written *Development* Plan

_____There is a written *strategic plan for development* that is guiding the *development* efforts at your school.

_____This written *strategic plan for development* has been created through the involvement of people – financial leaders, school leaders, alumni, parents, etc.

_____This written plan has priorities, goals, timeline and persons responsible.

_____The *core team* is working with those in charge of *development* in terms of implementation.

_____This Plan is being reviewed and updated on a monthly basis.

Possible Score: 15

Total Score: _____

Comments:____

Assessment Area 7: Identification and Engagement of People

_____The school continues to invite and involve over 100 new people to the *development/advancement* effort each year.

_____An excellent amount of time is being spent visiting with people "eyeball to eyeball" on a consistent (daily and weekly) basis.

_____There is an on-going people identification process in place.

_____School leaders (pastor, principal, president, school advisory council, development committees, *core team*) are making approximately 3-5 personal visits to new families, present school families, alumni, prospective financial leaders, new surfacing leaders, etc.) each month.

_____There is an organized, electronic and paper tracking system in place for all key publics of the school.

Possible Score: 15

Total Score: _____

Comments:____

Assessment Area 8: Public Relations and Image Building

_____There is an organized, written public relations and image building plan in place for the school. (This may be a component of the *strategic plan for development*).

_____School leaders are constantly being educated on their role as a "public relations agent" or ambassador.

_____The image of the school in the community is excellent.

_____The image of the school with feeder sources is excellent and constantly being improved.

_____The value of the school is known by the majority of the parents, alumni, staff and students.

_____The verbal and visual image (brand) of the school is clear to all internal publics and is being promoted.

Possible Score: 18

Total Score: _____

Comments:____

Assessment Area 9: Publications and Web Site

_____School publications project a positive, clear and consistent message about the school – its mission, message and brand.

_____Publications are completed and distributed in a timely manner.

_____The quality of the publications projects the kind of image that the school wants to project.

_____The publications for the school did undergo or will undergo an evaluation process before the end of the fiscal year.

_____The web site is used as a major communication vehicle for the school.

_____The web site is interactive and invites people to fill in forms, request information, and sign up for various activities.

_____People can offer financial gifts on the web site.

_____The web site is monitored and updated on a daily basis.

_____Information requested from the web site is responded to in a timely manner.

_____The web site is evaluated on a consistent basis by people who have expertise in that field of work.

_____The web site is strong enough to do such things as stream videos and handle payments to the annual fund and gifts to the capital campaign, etc.

_____The school takes advantage of social media in order to better communicate with its constituents.

Possible Score: 36

Total Score: _____

Comments:____

Assessment Area 10: Enrollment Management

_____The enrollment management efforts this school year are going to bring the desired number of students into the school for the next school year.

_____The enrollment management activities are organized and are producing results not only for this coming year but future ones.

_____The majority of the enrollment management activities center on personal attention.

_____The EM efforts emphasize getting prospective parents and students onto the campus for various functions and activities.

_____The *core team*, students, parents, faculty and staff of the school are involved in this effort.

_____The admissions process allows for a win-win partnership to be established at the beginning of the relationship.

_____The open house (s) was (were) successful this year.

Possible Score: 21

Total Score: _____

Comments:____

Assessment Area 11: Alumni Involvement

_____The school has an organized alumni effort in place – one that is working well.

_____The school has an organized class rep system.

_____The school has an alumni board or steering group in place.

_____The relationship between the alumni and the school is a good one.

_____The alumni supports the school through various *development* $$$ and fund-raising efforts.

_____The school is making strides in building relationships with out of town alumni.

_____The alumni activities at school are well attended and people seem to enjoy them.

Possible Score: 21

Total Score: _____

Comments:____

Assessment Area 12: Annual Fund

_____The annual fund will meet its goals ($$$ and people) this year and will be seen as a success.

_____The major gift component of the annual fund was a point of strong emphasis.

_____The number of people who gave gifts to the annual fund increased by 10% - 15% from last year to this year.

_____There was a lot of personal "eyeball to eyeball" work.

_____The amount of people to lead the annual fund increased by 10% - 15% from last year.

_____Donors believed the goals and case were clear and compelling.

_____You invited gifts of prayer, involvement and finance.

_____The annual fund this year retained 90%+ of the donors from last year.

Possible Score: 21

Total Score: _____

Comments:____

Assessment Area 13: Long Range Planning

_____The school has a long range, strategic plan in place – a comprehensive one that was created through the involvement of hundreds of people.

_____This long range, strategic plan addresses all major areas of the school.

_____There is a group of school leaders who are responsible for the implementation of the LRSP.

_____Those working in Catholic *development* are well aware of the plan's priorities, and they are able to articulate (in the written and spoken word) the value of this plan to the school's future.

_____There is adequate communication to all publics on the progress of the plan's implementation.

Possible Score: 15

Total Score: _____

Comments:____

Assessment Area 14: Role of the Staff

_____Those working in Catholic *development* have a regular communication system in place to let the faculty/staff and parish staff (if applicable) know what is going on with the *development* efforts.

_____Parish (if applicable) and school staff members are represented on the *core team* and any of the planning teams that are put together.

_____Staff members are consistently educated on the true meaning of Catholic *development*.

_____Staff members receive a monthly one page update from the "development office" about what is going on in *development*.

_____Those working in Catholic *Development* take the time to meet personally with school staff in order to understand what is going on in their areas.

Possible Score: 15

Total Score: _____

Comments:____

Assessment Area 15: Seeking Input

_____School leaders understand the value of "pipelining" to the people.

_____Regular, organized and objective instruments (surveys, questionnaires, etc.) are in place in order to seek input from parents, parishioners, faculty and staff, students, alumni and other key publics in the school.

_____The Catholic *development* leaders of the school host input sessions at least once per year for various constituent groups.

_____The input that is collected is compiled and organized in such a way to make it valuable to future planning and action.

_____Input (interviews, input sessions, surveys, questionnaires, flip chart sessions, assemblies, etc.) is seen as an excellent way to engage people into the life of the school.

Possible Score: 15

Total Score: _____

Comments:____

Assessment Area 16: Special Event Fund-Raisers

_____The school has a master plan for fund-raising events in place and there is an organized calendar to make sure the school does not host one fund-raiser after another.

_____The fund-raisers invite and involve new potential leaders for the school.

_____The fund-raising events are enjoyable to those working and organizing as well as those attending.

_____The parents, alumni, and other publics do not feel that the school is "nickel and diming" them with too many fund-raisers.

_____The fund-raising events raise good **net** dollars.

_____When applicable, the faculty and staff, parents, alumni, and others support the fund-raising events.

_____The school conducts 2-4 major fund-raisers each year and has gotten rid of many of the nickel and dime efforts.

Possible Score: 21

Total Score: _____

Comments:____

Assessment Area 17: Use of Technology

_____The Catholic *development* efforts have effective software that is being used to keep track of all ***publics*** of the school.

_____The Catholic *development* efforts effectively use e-mails as a way to communicate, realizing that e-mail cannot take the place of person to person and relationship building.

_____The Catholic *development* efforts conduct on-line surveys with such programs as Survey Monkey and others.

_____The Catholic *development* efforts are able to handle preparing camera-ready items such as brochures and one page newsletters.

_____People are able to give to your Catholic institution on-line.

_____The Catholic *development* efforts are creating newsletters to various constituent groups and e-mailing them out on a consistent basis.

Possible Score: 18

Total Score: _____

Comments:____

Assessment Area 18: Demographic Data

_____The people working in Catholic *development* understand the value of having the latest demographic data.

_____The Catholic *development* efforts are consistently gathering data in regards to baptisms, population trends, housing trends, zip code segmentations, information from the Chamber of Commerce, the diocese, real estate agencies, builders, and other sources.

_____Your Catholic institution is paying close attention to what this data is telling you in terms of shifts in population, shifts in feeder source enrollment, etc.

_____You are including people in your Catholic *development* efforts who have expertise in county planning, statistical analysis, real estate trends, etc.

_____Your Catholic institution is factoring this data into future planning.

Possible Score: 15

Total Score: _____

Comments:____

Assessment Area 19: Welcoming and Greeting

_____There is a culture of warmth and personal greeting that permeates your Catholic institution – one that begins with the leadership of the school.

_____There is a vibrant welcoming committee for your school – one that welcomes new families with personal outreach. (*Core team* members may chair this effort).

_____Your school has an effective parent buddy system in place so that every family has 1-2 "buddy" families who communicate with them 2-4 times per year.

_____There is a written action plan in place that drives the welcoming and greeting efforts of the school.

_____Those working in Catholic *development* understand the value of "customer service."

Possible Score: 15

Total Score: _____

Comments:____

Assessment Area 20: Community Involvement

_____The people working in your Catholic *development* efforts have an organized list of businesses and others in your community.

_____There is a consistent effort to communicate with these community members.

_____Businesses in your community are not "hounded" by different groups, clubs and organizations from your school asking them for money.

_____The Catholic *development* efforts are working hard to develop business partners.

_____Those working in Catholic *development* are able to clearly articulate the needs of the school to those business and community leaders.

Possible Score: 15

Total Score: _____

Comments:____

Assessment Area 21: Capital Campaign

_____The people working in your Catholic *development* efforts understand that a capital campaign takes months of planning and people building before it is ever launched.

_____The case for support of your capital campaign is strong, compelling, and shows a strong need.

_____You are working to build a strong infrastructure of people who will chair the campaign, head up the various divisions of the campaign, and also serve as team members.

_____Your capital campaign is an effort to reach out person to person and invite people to consider participating.

_____Your capital campaign invites gifts of prayer, gifts of involvement and gifts of financial participation.

_____One of the main goals of your capital campaign is 75%+ participation of your key constituent groups.

Possible Score: 18

Total Score: _____

Comments:____

Assessment Area 22: Financial Leaders

_____Those working in your Catholic *development* efforts have identified your Top 100+ which is a list of persons/families who are capable of considering a financial gift of $1,000+ in the annual fund.

_____There is a consistent effort to personally communicate with and seek to involve many of these financial leaders.

_____The pastor, principal, and/or president is aware of who these people are and work at building a climate of affirmation and appreciation.

_____Any time there is a discussion of persons and/or families who may be considered financial leaders, it is done with utmost confidentiality and professionalism, with no one's name ever mentioned publicly in a group of people.

Possible Score: 12

Total Score: _____

Comments:____

Assessment Area 23: Inviting the Gifts

_____In inviting people's participation in the annual fund, the capital campaign, the endowment campaign, or other *development* $$$ efforts, you are always inviting the three gifts of prayer, involvement and finance.

_____The pastor, principal and/or president is heavily involved in one on one visits to invite the gifts.

_____A minimum of 50 "eyeball to eyeball" visits are made by those working with the Catholic *development* efforts in your school each year.

_____Personal visitation and invitations to consider are seen as wonderful ways to invite input and build relationships.

_____Those working in Catholic *development* have been educated on what to say and what not to say in a one on one visit.

Possible Score: 15

Total Score: _____

Comments:____

Assessment Area 24: Planned Giving

_____There is a planned giving process in place with an organized and written plan of action.

_____There is a planned giving committee of some kind who is leading the way. (Possibly headed up by a *core team* member)

_____Those working in Catholic *development* have excellent planned giving literature for distribution.

_____There is a strong educational component built into the planned giving process.

_____The school has 2-3 planned giving experts (CPA, tax attorney, financial planner, etc.) who have volunteered their time and expertise.

Possible Score: 15

Total Score: _____

Comments:____

Assessment Area 25: Grant Writing

_____There is an organized grant writing process in place.

_____Key local, state, regional and national foundations/corporations have been identified for cultivation and submission of proposals.

_____One person, or a team of people, have been designated the grant writer.

_____These people have received the necessary training and education.

_____The school has been successful this past year in securing 2-3 grants or more.

_____The faculty and staff are directly involved in the process – offering suggestions for grant requests.

Possible Score: 18

Total Score: _____

Comments:____

Assessment Area 26: Memorial Giving

_____There is an organized memorial gifts program in place for your school.

_____There is written material available for those who wish to read more about your memorial gifts program.

_____There is an excellent recording and tracking system in place for those who do make memorial gifts.

_____There is consistent education and invitation to all publics to make a memorial gift – when appropriate.

_____When applicable, there are meaningful recognition vehicles in place for those who make memorial gifts.

Possible Score: 15

Total Score: _____

Comments:____

Assessment Area 27: Endowment Growth

_____There is an effective endowment growth plan in place for the school.

_____The endowment (corpus) is being fueled each year with new money.

_____There is coordination between the endowment efforts and the overall *development* efforts.

_____Consideration is given to include a percentage of the capital campaign and/or annual fund to endowment growth.

_____Consideration is also given to a campaign that is exclusively for endowment growth.

_____It is clear what specific endowment programs are available and this is published for all to understand.

Possible Score: 18

Total Score: _____

Comments:____

Assessment Area 28: On-Going Catholic *Development* Education

_____Those working in Catholic *development* are committed to on-going education by attending workshops, conventions, conferences, seminars, webinars, and other means of professional growth.

_____Money is budgeted to allow for this to happen.

_____Professional growth is encouraged by the leaders of the school.

_____The pastor, principal and/or president is also committed to continue to learn both the art and the science of Catholic *development*.

_____Groups of people from your school are encouraged to attend workshops, seminars, conventions, conferences, etc. together in order to learn as a team.

Possible Score: 15

Total Score: _____

Comments:____

Assessment Area 29: Re-charging the Battery

_____Those working in Catholic *development* understand the value of stepping back and looking at the big picture at least once a quarter – simply by asking *core team* members one question, "How are we doing so far this year?"

_____The pastor, principal and/or president understand that those working in *development* should not be expected to keep "office hours" from 9-5.

_____Because of evening and weekend work, down time is built into the schedules of those working in Catholic *development*.

_____Those working in Catholic *development* build into the budget the plan to get away overnight at least 1-2x per year for motivation and re-charging the battery.

Possible Score: 12

Total Score: _____

Comments:____

Assessment Area 30: Challenges and Future Initiatives

_____You have identified the main challenges you face in your *development/advancement* efforts for the future.

_____You have identified the main 8-10 focus areas for your *development/advancement* efforts in the next year.

_____You have clearly articulated the accomplishments of the *development/advancement* efforts for this year.

_____You have squared away what *development/advancement* office personnel you will need for the next year.

Possible Score: 12

Total Score: _____

Comments:____

Lesson 12: Create the Long-Range Strategic Plan for Your School.

"Without vision, we perish."
"If you always do what you've always done, you will always get what you've always gotten."

There are many types of planning processes that Catholic schools are presented with – from their diocesan or Catholic school office, from the state in which they reside, from regional or national agencies, and even from some outside firms. Some take the form of evaluations and accreditations; others take the form of five year planning efforts; and others are launched because school leaders want to build a stronger vision and plan for the future. Oftentimes, the latter effort produces the best results, because it is not mandated, and it usually grows out of a desire to improve.

"The solutions that you used to get you to where you are today, will not be the same solutions that will get you to where you want to be tomorrow."

"I plan to spend the rest of my life in the future, so I want to be reasonably sure of what kind of future it's going to be. That is my reason for planning."

"Insanity is doing the same thing over and over again and expecting the results to be different."

All of these above quotes call to mind the importance of planning for any Catholic school. We believe that there is a choice on how a Catholic school goes about planning for the future. Do you want to approach planning from a *development* (people involvement) stance or from a "let's get it done" stance? Is your planning effort going to involve just the leadership of your school, or is it going to reach out and invite 2nd, 3rd and 4th ripple people? Are you going to seek input from those with whom you feel comfortable, or are you going to invite those with various views and opinions to come to the table?

These are all valid questions, and you can tell from the way these questions are worded, what we believe. A planning effort needs to invite and engage people. If you are planning the future of your Catholic school, why limit your input to parents, board, faculty and staff, and alumni? Why not invite leaders from other schools? Why not invite experts in the fields of technology, academics, athletics, student life, finance, *development*, administration, and buildings and grounds? This is planning done from a *development* stance: inviting and engaging people to become part of your future.

Will they come and help you? This is a question we hear all over the country, and the answer is YES! People want to help, even if they do not "belong" to your school. Catholic schools can be the recipients of much wisdom if we open up our doors and invite people inside. Here are four key points to consider before you invite people to become involved:

1. Know why you are launching the planning process.
2. Make sure there is objectivity built into the process.

3. Make sure there is an outline that shows anyone how you will move forward.
4. Make sure you are prepared to hear and respect what others have to say – even if it is different from your own opinions.

Why not make a commitment to planning the future of your Catholic school for the next 1 – 3 – 5 years and beyond? Any time is a wonderful time to move ahead and put together a plan that is dynamic, visionary, and positive. Why be reactive when you can be proactive? The 12 basic components are not that difficult:

1. Assessment
2. Establishment of steering group
3. Research
4. Grass roots input (surveys, questionnaires, etc.)
5. SWOT (strengths, weaknesses, opportunities, and threats) analysis
6. Mission and vision
7. Planning areas
8. Articulation of key challenges
9. Invitation to many to help solve the challenges
10. Prioritization
11. Final Plan
12. Implementation

Through the years we have found that there are important steps to take that will move the planning process along for Catholic schools. Those steps are outlined in this lesson.

Step One: Steering Committee and School Assessment

- Form, educate and implement a *steering committee.*
- Create and implement a comprehensive communication and education plan on the strategic planning process.
- Collect, analyze, present and integrate quantitative and qualitative data.
    - Surveys (The Ultimate Question)
    - Questionnaires
    - Input Sessions

- Build the Planning Areas for the process around the *National Standards and Benchmarks for Effective Catholic Elementary and Secondary Schools.*
    - Mission and Catholic Identity
    - Academic Excellence
    - Governance and Leadership
    - Operational Vitality
- Have the *steering committee* identify planning area team members (10-15 per planning area) that will work with that specific planning area for 3-4 workshops.

Step Two: Planning Area Teams and Their Focus

- The planning area teams, chaired by 2-3 *steering committee* members, should work to accomplish the following:
    - Examine and possibly recreate the school's mission statement as the core to the planning process;
    - Conduct a SWOT analysis (Strengths, Weaknesses, Opportunities and Threats) of that planning area;
        - Mission and Catholic identity
        - Academic excellence
        - Governance and leadership
        - Operational vitality
    - Create a Purpose Statement for that Planning Area;
        - "The purpose of the academic excellence planning area is to create a plan that will . . . ."
    - Create 4-6 Challenges per planning area – based upon the assessment work, the SWOT, and the discussions with the *steering committee;*
        - "How can we . . . ."
    - Offer solutions to the challenges surfaced by the planning area team based around the SMART formula, where the solutions are:
        - S = Strategic
        - M = Measurable
        - A = Achievable
        - R = Relevant
        - T = Time-driven

Step Three: Long-Range Strategic Plan Draft

- Based upon the challenges and solutions offered through planning team meetings, create the draft of the Long-Range Strategic Plan (LRSP).
- The draft LRSP should have the following components:
    - Mission/vision statement
    - Four planning areas
        - Purpose Statement
        - Challenges
        - Strategic solutions
            - S = Strategic
            - M = Measurable
            - A = Achievable
            - R = Relevant
            - T = Time-driven

Step Four: School-Wide Congress

- The *steering committee* and the planning area teams should come together to convene a school-wide congress.
- In addition to the planning area teams, invitations should go out to those throughout the area (100 mile radius of the school) with specific areas of expertise. For example:
    - **Operational Vitality Planning Area** -- delegates may include CPAs, financial planners, university CFOs, development officers on all levels, etc.
    - **Mission and Catholic Identity Planning Area** – delegates may include pastors, directors of religious education, theology teachers, campus ministers, etc.
- The purpose of the congress will be to divide delegates according to planning areas and have them solve the challenges for that planning area. Having been part of well over 100 of these congresses, I can testify that they are among the most exciting events your school will ever host. The formula of bringing together people with objectivity to work with people who are already involved can be dynamic.

Step Five: The Final Long-Range Strategic Plan and Implementation

- After the congress, the administration and the *steering committee* should create the final long-range strategic plan document. This document should articulate the priorities and the implementation plan to insure the future of the school for many years to come.

- The final plan should have the following components:
  - Mission and vision and guiding principles
  - Process and methodology
  - Data analysis
  - Planning areas
    - Purpose statement
    - SWOT
    - Challenges
      - Strategic Initiatives
    - Priorities
    - Recommendations
- With the implementation of the long-range strategic plan, it will be important to assure that the following components are established:
  - Communication of the plan
  - Implementation teams for each planning area of the plan
  - Establishment of the sustainability standards
  - Measurements and benchmarks for each strategic initiative of the long-range strategic plan

In terms of Catholic school *development*, having a vision and a plan that can be articulated is so important to future success. We encourage each and every Catholic school to create this dynamic plan of action.

Lesson 13: Set Up Your Development Director to Succeed.

All across America today there are hundreds of Catholic school and/or parish development directors who are making exciting things happen in their ministry. Some are one person "shops" and others have 2 or 3 or even more in their *development/advancement* office. Some of these folks have been at this for years, and many are brand new to the world of Catholic school *development.* In ISPD's work throughout the country, we have consulted with and/or "work-shopped" with hundreds of development officers. In one workshop I recently conducted we had 17 development directors present – from elementary schools, high schools, regional schools, and K-12 schools with similar challenges, similar frustrations, and similar cries for help.

Years ago when I was a development director at a Catholic high school, I often bemoaned the fact that I had very little guidance, no outside professional help, a broad lack of understanding by the board of what *development* really was, and a long list of expectations that basically translated into three words: "Raise More Money!"

Catholic school development directors usually last 2.3 years. This statistic comes from working with approximately 250+ each year through our on-site consulting, workshops, and webinars. We find ourselves always asking, "How long have you been in this position?" or "How long did she/he last?" What we also find is that many Catholic school development directors do not last longer for seven reasons:

1. Lack of understanding by the administration, board, decision makers, and even the development officer that Catholic school *development* needs to be seen as a system of processes built around the themes of people engagement and resource development;
2. No written, formal, strategic plan with priorities and benchmarks from which to operate;
3. No on-going professional training where growth is encouraged and tracked over a period of years;
4. Everything being measured by the amount of money that is to be raised;
5. Constantly running one fund-raising event after the other;
6. Lack of realization that Catholic school *development* takes 2-4 years to gain the "legs" it needs to be successful;
7. Little time spent to "re-charge the battery."

With the above in mind, we would like to offer some tips on how development officer(s) can succeed.

1. Get trained and constantly grow in your ministry.

- There are many opportunities for growth in this ministry. There are workshops and webinars offered throughout the country. Your Diocese may offer in-services; the NCEA Convention has wonderful presenters and presentations; there are many *development/advancement* publications from NCEA. Explore the opportunities to network with other professionals in your area.

- Going to a 1-2 day workshop simply gives you a framework. Please remember there is the "art" of Catholic *development* and there is "science" of Catholic *development*. The art (people management) is learned through experience; that is the main teacher. The science is learned through experience and education; the science is all the processes that make up the world of Catholic *development*:
    - How to conduct an annual fund;
    - How to host an open house;
    - How to promote a special event fund-raiser;
    - How to invite the gifts;
    - How to run a major gift reception;
    - How to set up a planned giving effort;
    - How to implement a *core team*;
    - How to create the long-range strategic plan;
- The list of Catholic school *development* processes goes on and on.

2. Educate your leaders.

- We believe that pastors, principals, board members, etc. should know what Catholic school *development* is and what it is not. We encourage you to get your leaders to workshops; send them e-mails; forward news clippings; encourage articles, webinars and books; get them to network with others who understand.
- As part of your survival, your leadership (which is always changing) needs to be educated constantly.

3. Make personal visits every week.

- Please, get out of the office and have a cup of coffee or "eyeball to eyeball" meeting with 5 new people each week. This is a people business; this is not a computer lab.
- Seek their advice; ask for input; invite their participation in the Catholic school *development* process.

4. Work from a written plan of action.

- This is the main reason development directors do not succeed. There is no written plan of action. There is a lot of, "Well, I think you should be doing this and that." But, no one ever says how. A written plan of action that uses the SMART formula will always lead to success.

- The strategic action must:
    - S: Be strategic and begin with an action verb.
    - M: Be measurable so you will know how you are doing or did.
    - A: Be achievable.
    - R: Be relevant to your situation.
    - T: Be driven by a timetable.

5. Encourage consideration of three years.

- When you accept your new position as development officer or when it is time for renewal, ask for the consideration of three years. It takes that long to DEVELOP and ADVANCE.

6. Bond with the staff.

- It is so important that you understand one tenet that we have already stated in this book: The most important group of people to bond and get along with is the faculty/staff. They live the mission every day; they are in touch with your "customers' every day. Please bond with them consistently.

7. Assemble and work with the *core team*.

- We have referred a lot to the *core team* concept in this book, and we have worked hard in putting hundreds of these in place. They are the "lifeline" for your success. Please discuss this more and bring these 15-18 people into your world. Please note: The *core team* concept is not just for new Catholic school *development* efforts; it is for every school, no matter how advanced you may be. Some of the best *core team* efforts are with Catholic schools that have had *development* in place for 20+ years.

8. Word process a monthly update.

- Please let your "internal markets" know what you are doing. It helps to word process a one page, one side monthly *update* simply using bullet points to list the many processes and initiatives you are working on. Hard copy, electronic copy – it makes no difference. This should go to administration, board, council, staff, and key leadership groups.

9. Listen, Listen, Listen.

- *Belonging leads to believing*. People feel that sense of belonging when they are invited to share their ideas. By listening, we really say to people that we care about their perspectives, opinions and stories. We make them feel they belong.

10. Make healthy choices.

- Been at it a while and still banging your head up against a brick wall because of a lack of leadership or lack of understanding of what you are doing? Usually once or twice a month, we run across this scenario, and as we have said many times, (when Catholic development officers are in a "no win" situation), "Life is about choices." There are thousands of outstanding Catholic leaders all across America, and yet there are a few who believe that the only management method is, "My way or the highway." Total boss management. In 25+ years in this consulting profession, I have never seen Catholic school *development* flourish when that style of management is present.

11. Reward yourself.

- The battery needs to be re-charged. The tank needs to be re-fueled. Great Catholic leaders who "die" in the heat of battle because of stress are doing themselves a disservice. Four statements we always make – much to the chagrin of *development* leaders:
    - Everyone is replaceable.
    - Let go; you simply cannot do everything. Delegate, delegate, delegate! Please don't play the victim role. There are "troops" willing and waiting to come to your side if you will only let them.
    - "It's okay to make a mistake!"
    - Please take some time off – physically, emotionally, mentally and spiritually.

12. Be responsible for but don't guard your kingdom.

- There are wonderful resource people that you can count on – both within your community and outside of it. Please work hard to establish a system that invites input and expertise. The greatest legacy you can leave is a Catholic school *development* system that works – even without you.

Lesson 14: Create a Master Plan for Your Fund-Raising Events.

How many times have we heard the statement from Catholic school parents, alums, students, and others, "All they do is 'nickel and dime' us to death at that school. It is one fund-raiser after another, after another."

Or, the potential $1,000 major donor to the school Annual Fund says to the principal, "Bob, I would love to participate, but my wife just bought two raffle calendars for $100. We already gave."

Or, the parents of the quarterback on the football team, who are potential $50,000 lead donors for the school's capital campaign say to the president after he invites their gift, "Father, we would love to get involved, but we just gave $5,000 to the football program when Coach Stevens asked us to help pay for the new scoreboard."

Stories like this go on and on in Catholic institutions. As we have said in recent newsletters, the financial model of tuition, subsidy and fund-raisers leaves a lot to be desired. Although we have explained it before, I do believe it is worthwhile to explain again: There is a huge difference between fund-raising $$$ and *development* $$$. Let's look.

When we speak of fund-raising $$$ we mean "buy and sell." I am going to sell you a BINGO card, and you will buy it. I am going to sell you a raffle calendar or a Christmas tree or Christmas wrapping paper, or a Heath candy bar or a T-shirt or a raffle ticket or the sponsorship of the 18th hole of the golf tournament. These are special event fund-raisers – car washes, walkathons, washathons, etc. Most of the people who buy the ticket are not interested in the vision, mission, goals, and plans for the future of your Catholic school. They simply want their wrapping paper.

Is there anything wrong with this? No. However, it does become a problem when we do one fund-raiser right after another.

Now, let's talk about *development* $$$. This is philanthropic giving; this is stewardship; this is investing in your Catholic institution and expecting nothing in return. No wrapping paper, no candy, no popcorn. People who think this way invest in the annual fund, the capital campaign, the endowment campaign, the memorial gift program, and/or consider a planned gift for the parish. *Buy/ sell vs. being a steward.*

We do recognize that shifting from a fund-raising mentality to a *development* mentality is difficult. Change is onerous. A friend of mine once told me this story.

"The first time I was invited to my future in-laws' house for Sunday dinner, they served roast beef. I was engaged to their daughter and at the Sunday dinner I met my wife's grandmother. When they served the roast beef, I noticed that both ends were cut off. I thought this was unusual. So I asked my fiancé if, when she made roast beef, did she cut off both ends. She said she did. I then asked my future mother in law if, when she made roast beef, did she, in fact, cut off both ends? She said, 'Yes, of course I do'.

"I then asked Grandma if when she made roast beef if she cut off both ends, and she said, 'Of course I do'.

"I then asked, 'Why would you cut off both ends of the roast beef'?

"Grandma replied, 'I never had a big enough pot'!"

For no apparent reason, we continue to do things without any reason, except, "That is the way we have always done it." Some school fund-raisers are no different.

Through the years we have heard the same thing: "We are doing too many fund-raisers, and we have no control over who does what. Plus, how in the world are we going to tell the band boosters that they can't raise money, or tell the cheerleaders that they cannot hold bake sales and car washes? And, are you going to tell the athletic boosters that they can't sell ads for the football program all over town?"

The sad thing is that this way of thinking is built around a year to year modus operandi. This makes it difficult for the investment processes like the annual fund to even breathe. And, the thought of a capital campaign amid all of this is way too much to think about. It will hardly get out of the blocks.

So, how do we break the cycle? How do we stop the short-term thinking? How do we approach all of this from a systemic point of view? Although we referred to this in Lesson 5, we now would like to go into more detail.

1. Visually, create a chart on poster paper. (***See ISPD Fund-Raising Chart***). Using a chart, write down EVERY fund-raiser that your school conducts. This includes all clubs, organizations, sports teams, school sponsored events, etc. On this chart have the following categories:
    - Name of the fund-raiser
    - Time of the year
    - How long it took to organize and conduct
    - Gross amount collected
    - Net amount raised
    - How many people it took to organize it
    - Approximate number of "people hours" it took to make this event happen
    - Who was asked for the money
        - Parents
        - Parishioners
        - Faculty and Staff
        - Students
        - Alumni
        - Friends
        - Others:

2. Begin educating your leadership groups on the present reality.
   - Present this visual to them and explain the challenges.
   - Have your boards, your coaches, your faculty/staff, your student leaders, your PTA, and others realize how counter-productive it is to "nickel and dime" people.
   - Explain the differences between Catholic *development* and fund-raising events.
   - Explain the need for change by all, and that by a certain date you will have in place a process for groups, clubs, and organizations to apply to conduct a fund-raiser.
   - Explain that you are going to center the *development* and/or *advancement* efforts around the annual fund and 3-4 excellent fund-raisers that: a. Raise good net dollars; b. Build new leadership; c. Bring people together.
3. Put together a committee of 5-6 people who will screen, reject and/or approve all applications for clubs, groups, and organizations to conduct fund-raisers. Include in this group:
   - Principal
   - Person working in *development/advancement*
   - Parent leader
   - Board member
4. By (whatever date you establish), present the application form to all people at the school, indicating that any and all applications need to be handed in by (date).
5. Have the Committee meet and select the fund-raising events that will be accepted for the next school year. Once again, the annual fund is NOT a "fund-raising event." It is "*development* $$$."

The leaders of the schools and/or parishes who move in this direction (and it may take longer than one year) are also aware of the financial needs of the clubs and organizations. Oftentimes, percentages of the annual fund are devoted to those groups, and/or percentages of net dollars raised in the fund-raisers are allocated to clubs and organizations. The bottom line is this: if ALL fund-raising efforts are not coordinated throughout the SYSTEM, it will be difficult for the school to be successful in moving forward with *development* $$$ (annual fund, capital campaign, major gift work, etc.)

Change is onerous, and many times we don't change unless the pain gets so severe that we are forced to change. We believe the pain in Catholic institutions is acute. If old ways of thinking and doing the same old thing over and over again are allowed to prevail, we will continue to get the same short term results.

"Jesus told them of this parable, 'No one tears a patch from a new garment and sews it on an old one. If he does, he will have torn the new garment, and the patch from the new will not match the old. And no one pours new wine into old wineskins. If he does, the new wine will burst the skins, the wine will run out and the wineskins will be ruined. No, new wine must be poured into new wineskins'."

Luke 5:36-39

ISPD Fund-Raising Chart

KEY

P - Parents
PR - Parishioners
A - Alum
F - Faculty
S - Students
PP - Past Parents
F - Friends
BC - Board/Council
GP - Grandparents
B - Businesses
G - General Public

	Sponsor	Month	Gross $	Net $	# of People	Hours	P	PR	A	F	S	PP	GP	B	F	BC	G
FR1																	
FR2																	
FR3																	
FR4																	
FR5																	
FR6																	
FR7																	
FR8																	
FR9																	
FR10																	
FR11																	
FR12																	
FR13																	
FR14																	
FR15																	
FR16																	
FR17																	
FR18																	
FR19																	
FR20																	
FR21																	
FR22																	
FR23																	
FR24																	
FR25																	

Through the years we have found that it is important to take the time – usually over a period of 1-2 weeks – and really assess what is going well, what needs to improved, what needs to be dropped, what needs to be tweaked, and what needs to be added. Two areas that we caution Catholic schools not to fall prey to:

1. Some Catholic schools – over the years -- keep adding events and activities. Sometimes these events are important and make a positive difference to the *development* operation, and sometimes they are just there because, "We've always done that." The assessment, done correctly, allows a Catholic school to look closely at what is really necessary.
2. In assessing your *development* operation, please do not let 1-2 people do it all. It is not good enough for just the principal or the development director to assess everything. "Talk to the customer." We encourage you to get the feedback from a group of people, and we do encourage the use of the assessment exercise in the Addendum of the book.

Lesson 15: Promote the Belief That Enrollment Management Is Everyone's Responsibility.

As the years have unfolded since we began our *development* journey, I would have to argue that Catholic school enrollment continues to surface as the # 1 challenge for the majority of Catholic schools throughout the country. Hundreds and hundreds of Catholic schools have closed since the turn of the century and while not all of those closings have been due to shrinking enrollment, many have closed because of lack of students.

In a recent workshop, I made the statement that enrollment management (once called student recruitment) is the single most important area that a Catholic school should address. This statement was met with some push back. Some of the comments I heard were:

"That is ridiculous. The most important thing for a Catholic school to address is our Catholic identity."

"What? The quality of leadership for our Catholic school is the most important area."

"Our parents want technology. Granted, enrollment is important but having that new technology lab is going to bring in students."

These are all valid statements; however, I still stand pat on the original thought: enrollment management is the single most important area that a Catholic school should address. There will be no Catholic mission to teach and live out if there are no students. There will be no need to hire anyone as the principal if the enrollment is too low to maintain existence. And, the new technology lab is useless if there are not students to sit behind those computers and laptops.

Enrollment management is everyone's responsibility in a Catholic school. This is not just the job for the principal or the director of enrollment management or the admissions director, or the director of marketing. This is everyone's job if that Catholic school is going to prevail and not just survive. This is why it is so important that the leaders of every Catholic school educate everyone – board members, faculty members, staff members, parent leaders, student leaders – on their role in helping with and supporting the enrollment management efforts. From Day 1, any person who becomes involved in a specific Catholic school should be educated on the following:

- Top 10 selling points for that Catholic school;
- The meaning and understanding of the value of the enrollment management efforts of that Catholic school;
- His or her specific role in the enrollment management efforts.

In this lesson, we would like to offer 10 observations we have made in Catholic schools that have successful enrollment management efforts in place – beginning with # 10.

#10: The school understands the demographics of the educational marketplace and promotes its competitive advantage with attractive materials and targeted, compelling messaging – especially its top 10 selling points.

#9: Those in the entire school community (students, parents, faculty, staff, administration, alumni, board, etc.) understand they must take ownership of enrollment management and understand the roles they play. (For example, participating in creating the top 10 selling points).

#8: They understand that enrollment management and "customer service" are linked together. The faculty and staff understand the value of high level parent and student satisfaction. This translates into positive self-promotion.

#7: They understand that they must pay close attention to financial aid, tuition assistance, tuition rates and all streams of revenue. These are key factors in the enrollment process.

#6: They understand that enrollment management is an exciting process. In these schools, there is a positive attitude throughout the campus, and staff members are thrilled with promotional events, the open house and giving campus tours. Interested parents serve to validate the good work of these folks.

#5: They understand that enrollment management is about people fuel. There is an active enrollment management team in place who meets monthly to execute key strategies. There are also many people serving on marketing teams, acting as ambassadors for the school – all working together.

#4: They understand that there needs to be a marketing plan in place with clear goals, roles and responsibilities. Everyone is trained to execute key marketing strategies – from the front office to volunteers. There is a marketing budget and these schools take full advantage of word-of-mouth advertising from raving fans. Every prospect is important and there is a systematic follow-up process in place with frequent, compelling, benefit-focused messages that build relationships.

#3: They understand the value of ongoing evaluation with surveys, benchmarks and the need to implement innovative ideas. They work from the inside – out to address key issues and challenges. There is a culture of trust, innovation and total quality.

#2: They understand that technology is an essential tool. Utilizing electronic and mobile platforms, these schools establish a process of systematic and seamless communication with both prospective and current parents in a personalized manner that cultivates quality relationships. The website is a 24-7 marketing tool and social media is embraced as a vital method of contact and connection.

#1: They understand that enrollment management is their number 1 priority – the lifeblood of the school. These are schools of excellence. Every action and activity is executed at high levels of professionalism. They recognize that by embracing change, a positive result can be realized. People are treated with respect and challenges are viewed as opportunities. They understand that they must be attractive in order to attract others. Thoughtful attention is placed on the details – from the state of the parking lot to the actions in and out of the classroom. The mission of the school is paramount and a bright future is on the horizon.

Throughout the book, we keep referring to the top 10 selling points; here is what we mean. How many people actively promote your Catholic school? How many people know exactly what to promote and market year to year?

The most effective way of sharing the messages of a Catholic school is "eyeball to eyeball" – one-on-one, small group or large group. Interaction and relationship building are the keys to building your brand and your position. We believe that every Catholic school should have ten key points to promote, sell, and/or "shout out" to all "publics" every year. These ten points of the message need to be built, and the key ambassadors for the school should be invited to create them. Who are the key ambassadors?

- Administration
- Board
- Faculty and staff
- Those working in *development* and enrollment management
- Student leaders
- Parent leaders
- Alumni leaders

Remember: These key ambassadors need to be invited to share the messages of the brand, and although these ambassadors work with open house and on boards, plus many other areas, this whole concept of ambassadors works so well when every person knows the 10 key points to sell.

Let's look at how your school can develop these top 10 selling points and thereby build up the "critical mass."

1. School leaders (administration, *core team*, *advancement*/enrollment management directors, etc.) should meet with each key ambassador group. Let's use the faculty and staff of a Catholic school as an example.
2. In a brainstorming sessions, with flip chart paper, spend 10-15 minutes getting ideas up on the flip chart by asking one question: What are the most important items we need to promote and sell about our Catholic school?
3. Write all of these ideas down on flip chart paper. Post these flip charts throughout the room. Let's say that this group came up with 28 ideas.
4. Tell the group that you are going to "multi-vote." With 28 ideas, simply divide that number in ½ and tell your group that they need to select (in no order of importance) the 14 ideas they like the best. Allow them time to get up and mingle and go to each sheet of paper and look at all of the ideas. Each person needs to select 14 ideas.
5. When everyone is ready, the facilitator needs to go down the list of 28 and ask with each idea, "How many voted for # 1?" Write down the number of votes next to #1 and then do that for all 28. The top 10 vote getters are your top ten.
6. Follow the same process with every key group: board, parent leaders, student leaders, etc. You will come away with the top 10 from 5-6 different groups, but we can assure you of one thing: many of these ideas will be the same.
7. These need to be taken back to the leadership group (administration, board, development

officers, etc.) and edited. The final list should have no duplications. This leadership group then multi-votes the final list to get the final top 10.

8. NOTE: One question that always comes up is: Aren't there different messages for different audiences? Yes, there are, and those can be developed separately. What you are creating here is the top 10 no matter who the audience is.

These top 10 selling points need to be used throughout the fiscal year in many ways. However, the main point to remember is: Make hundreds of cards for all of your key ambassadors – usually 4" x 6" works well. All ambassadors need to receive 10-25 of these cards, with contact information on them. Now, all ambassadors can share the same messages:

- In informal conversations
- In answering telephones
- In social settings
- In speaking with new parents
- At an open house
- At all of the many ways Catholic schools get people on their campus
- At donor functions
- And, the list goes on and on
- NOTE: These are VOCAL messages.

Why should selling/marketing/promoting a Catholic school rest only with the people who are assigned to market it? Why should people only delve into what to sell before an open house? How valuable would it be to have hundreds of ambassadors for your brand each year? When all the messengers share the same message, then critical mass takes over and a Catholic school grows in reputation. Enrollment management is everyone's responsibility.

Lesson 16: Understand the Value of Your WOW!

Back years ago, I was asked by NCEA to write one of their fastback books on how to create newsletters, brochures, mission statements, promotional materials, etc. Of course, back then we did not have the technology we had today, yet there were a lot of excellent items being churned out on the old iMac by many development directors. Before writing the book which was titled *Catholic School Publications: Unifying the Image*, one of the exercises I undertook was to write to over 300 Catholic schools and request information – their mission statements, their promo materials, their school brochures, their annual reports, their newsletters, etc. What I got back was very interesting. While many had excellent material, many Catholic schools kept saying the same thing over and over. I must have read "quality Catholic education" over 200 times. It became apparent that the challenge to be distinctive was just that – a challenge.

Since that beginning year, I have continued to ask that question: What distinguishes your Catholic school (or parish) from others? By asking this, I do not mean what makes you better. I simply mean: What is your WOW!? What will draw people to your Catholic school?

At many of our workshops, we keep asking over and over again: What is your WOW!? The main answers we continue to get are:

- Quality academic program
- Outstanding students
- Excellent family-like atmosphere
- Wonderful parents
- New laptop computers for students
- Great community outreach program
- # 1 in the state in volleyball for three years straight
- Dynamic priest
- Clean and safe campus

These are all excellent "brag points" as we call them. However, I do not immediately label them as WOW!. So many Catholic schools and parishes can point to the above highlights and say, "We have that."

Your WOW is tour-able; it can be seen and felt; it distinguishes you from everyone else. Sometimes the WOW! comes from history or culture or location or programs or personnel. Most of the time it is very creative, and it usually takes months of discussion to settle on what it is or what it can be.

Three examples of WOW!:

1. De La Salle High School in New Orleans, LA. The leadership of DLS, led by Dr. Michael Guillot, has created four classrooms of the future. All of them are built around the four C's:

Creativity, Collaboration, Critical Thinking, and Communication. You walk into one of these classrooms and your response is WOW! Not only is this wonderful for touring prospective families or showing to key donors or impressing the alumni with a school on the move, but the use of the 21st century classrooms by the students at De La Salle is remarkable. These rooms are in constant use.

2. Rayne Catholic Elementary in Rayne, LA. This is a small southwest Louisiana town. The school buildings look old, and when you drive up to the campus you know that you are looking at a campus that has many years of wear. However, once you get out of your car and walk into the school buildings, the place comes alive with colors and signs, and you feel you are at Disneyworld. The place sparkles; posters and arrows point the way – hundreds of them with every color of the rainbow. They have taken an aging facility and turned it into a place of excitement. Within five minutes, I was uttering that word again, "WOW!"

3. Scecina Memorial Catholic High School in Indianapolis, IN. I have had the pleasure of working with Joe Therber and his leadership team at Scecina for the past 3-4 years. Ever since I stepped foot in the building, I have always asked Joe, "Where is your WOW?" Joe and some of his administrative team even came down to De La Salle High School in New Orleans and saw the classrooms of the future. They saw that WOW!, but it wasn't their WOW!. As with attendees who come to our workshops who cannot answer the WOW! question, Joe and his team were challenged to come up with their WOW!. Recently, I arrived for our day-long consultation. I walked into the main hallway, and there it was. From floor to ceiling was a mural that went for yards and yards down the hallway depicting the history and the life of Father Thomas Scecina, the namesake of the school. The pictorial and the written stories of this World War II chaplain who perished at sea with prisoner of war soldiers are breathtaking. In addition, more murals have been added depicting the history of this school. Classes can come and learn; prospective families can come and stand in awe. Alumni can come back and be part of the legacy. It is almost like going to the World War II Museum in New Orleans – the pictures and the captions are that good. WOW!

What is your WOW!?

Lesson 17: Emphasize the Importance of the Annual Fund.

As we all know, an annual fund is a process which consistently (each year) solicits gifts from all of its various constituencies. It is more than just a fund campaign. It is a coordinated, concentrated effort on the part of the school to plan one major, professional effort which can produce better results than many small campaigns. It involves good organization, strong case points (which grow out of the case statement for the school), goals, prospects, volunteers, a timetable, many ways of communication with donors, invitations, accurate records, recognition, evaluation and planning for the next year's annual fund.

There are five requisites for a successful Annual Fund:

- Part of the on-going *development* system of processes
- Specific stated purposes
- Enhancement of the school programs
- Assignment to a specific time period
- Strong case points (where the money is going)

We have said many times: The annual fund is the single most important *development* $$$ process that a Catholic school can embark upon. It becomes the backbone for all *development* $$$ that come into the school.

It is not the purpose of this lesson to teach the annual fund process. However, there are lessons we have learned within this Lesson # 17 that we believe are important, so we are going to zero in on what we believe are the top 10 in terms of "must do" items for a successful annual fund. This allows us to focus on these points and encourage you to integrate them – when possible – into the annual fund process in which you are presently working or will be working in the future.

#1: Invite Three Gifts.

- As we have said many times, invite three gifts and not just one. We encourage you to invite the Gift of Prayer, the Gift of Service (Involvement) and the Gift of Financial Participation. In a Catholic school, we believe it is important to make sure that Gifts of Prayer and Gifts of Service are invited; they become major "pillars" of our role as Catholic stewards.
- In order to do that, we suggest that you put that language on your Intention Card:

Gift of Prayer (Please check what you intend to do).

___ Daily, pray the Annual Fund Prayer.

___ Participate in Adoration Chapel as an adorer.

___ Offer daily prayer for the realization of long-range vision.

___ Daily, pray the rosary.

___ Attend one extra Mass per month.

___ Other:____

- **Gift of Involvement/Service (Time, Talent, Wisdom and Expertise)**

  ___ Annual Fund leadership -- Specific Role ______________________

  ___ Gifts of Expertise and Wisdom you wish to share: ______________________

  ___ Host a reception for the Annual Fund.

  ___ Be an Ambassador for the Annual Fund.

  ___ Help in the Development Office.

- **Gift of Financial Participation**
  - Financial Gift: $__________________
  - Enclosed: ______________________
  - Divide into:
    - Monthly payments
    - Quarterly payments
    - Semi-annual payments
    - Annual payment

#2: Articulate Clear Case Points.

- The most successful annual funds always have very clear "case points" on where the money will be going. Build a covered walkway, fund the first year of the school's *development* office, purchase new microscopes for the science lab, and landscape the front entrance to the parish – these are all specific items to which people will relate. We suggest that you not offer restrictive gifts, but that you list the 3-4-5-6 items that you wish to fund with the gift of financial participation.

#3: Invite Annual Fund Chairs and Associate Chairs.

- We strongly suggest that your annual fund have a chair couple that will be in charge of this year's annual fund and an associate chair couple that will be in charge of next year's annual fund. People want to know who the leaders are.
- We like the couple configuration. It is not vital for success, but it does allow one of the spouses to attend a meeting if the other is not available.
- Annual fund chairs do three things: organize, communicate and motivate – and that is a lot.

#4: Move to "Eyeball to Eyeball."

- Whenever possible, invite the gifts "eyeball to eyeball" and not through the mail or over the phone or on the web or through e-mail. Person-to-person will give you the best results.
- One-on-one meetings, small group receptions in homes, receptions at the school, get-togethers in restaurants are all effective.
- In many ways, your success will be determined by the number of people you personally invite "eyeball to eyeball."

#5: Recognize All Participants.

- In your recognition methods, please make sure that all people who turned in their Intention Card are recognized – alphabetically.
- The gifts may be prayer and/or service and/or financial participation, but the bottom line is all people should be recognized and appreciated equally.

#6: Understand the Annual Fund as Part of the Development System.

- As we have said many times, an annual fund needs to be one of the most important processes in the Catholic *development* system. By viewing *development* as a means to invite and involve and engage people in a meaningful way, your school needs to reach out and engage people and invite them to offer their gifts. That is a major objective of Catholic school *development*, and the annual fund is the perfect process to invite those three gifts.

#7: Create a Division Structure to the Annual Fund.

(***See Annual Fund Concept Chart***).

- An annual fund works well when there are two overall chairs and there are chairs of each division of the process.
- We invite you to consider the following divisions:
    - Major Gift Division
    - Leadership Gift Division (board, faculty and staff)
    - Parent Gift Division
    - Parishioner Gift Division (if applicable)
    - Alumni(ae) Gift Division
    - Friends Gift Division (past parents, grandparents and friends)
    - Business Community Gift Division

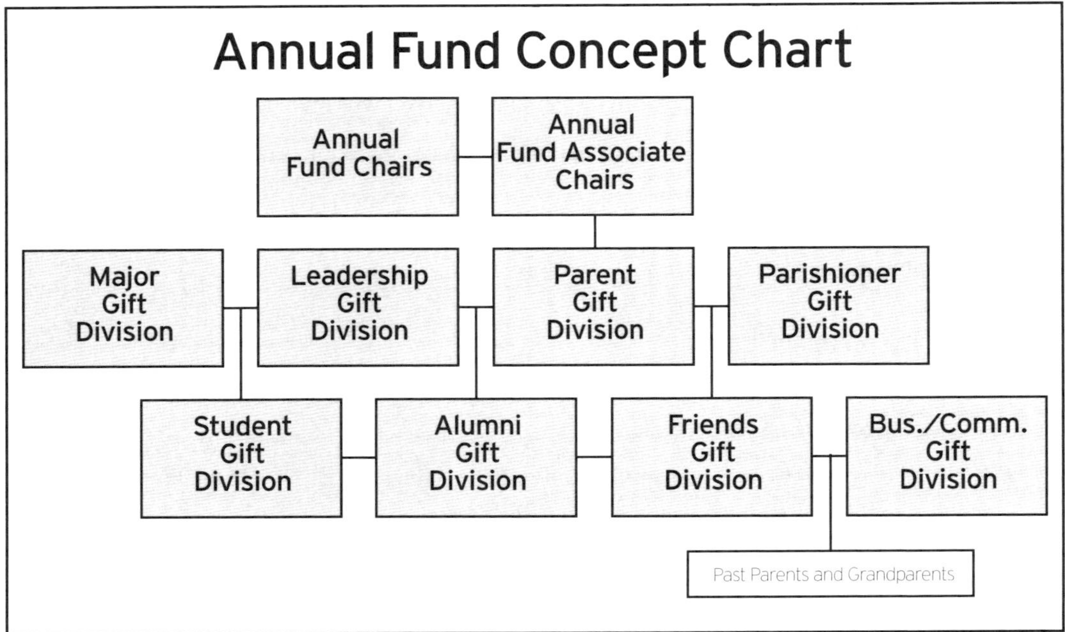

#8: Measure Your Annual Fund.

- Make sure there is an assessment process each year for your annual fund, and we suggest not to be so quick to judge the annual fund on how many dollars were raised.
- The annual fund should be evaluated and some key questions should be:
    - How much did our participation rate increase from last year to this one?
    - Did we retain 90%+ of our participants from last year?
    - Did we increase our participation by 15%+?
    - How many people gave the three gifts?
    - Do we know why participants who tuned in their intention cards last year did not turn in one this year?

#9: Implement the Major Gift Division.

- In terms of gifts of finance, the major gift division is the most important. This division usually invites people who could possibly consider a financial gift of $1,000+ each year.
- All of these should be "eyeball to eyeball," and with as many as possible a specific amount – such as $1,000+ should be suggested.
- You can have success in this division if you do one-on-one work or host a major gift reception or home reception or have the pastor-president-principal personally invite the gifts.
- In terms of dollars raised, it is not uncommon for the major gift division to raise 60% or more of the total amount needed.

#10: P-D-S-A: Plan-Do-Study-Adjust

- At the heart of the tools of Total Quality Management is the P-D-S-A process. This stands for Plan then Do then Study then Adjust. As simple as it sounds, it takes a shift in culture to think like this.
- The first step is to PLAN. A written plan for the annual fund is a must.
- The second step is to DO. In other words, work the plan.
- The third step is to STUDY. This mean to carefully study, evaluate and assess the annual fund at year's end. Know what went well and what did not.
- The fourth step is ADJUST. In those areas that were not successful, adjust your plan. For those areas where you need to add new steps, then go ahead and do so. If your annual fund structure is ready, then create your written plan and DO it.

Obviously, there are other key tenets, but we feel these ten focus on the areas we believe will help you enhance or begin your annual fund. As we said in the beginning of this lesson: The annual fund is the single most important *development* $$$ effort a Catholic school can ever do.

Lesson 18: Emphasize Win-Win with Your Alumni(ae) Base.

Laying the Groundwork: The First Areas to Address

Alums are so important to the development of a Catholic school; in many schools they are the undiscovered gem of many resources. While high schools and elementary schools are different in their approaches and their processes, the fact remains that the success of a Catholic school *development* effort is going to greatly depend upon the alum base.

The main focus for alums is identification of who is who. Without an accurate and comprehensive database, the alumni effort could be limited. Great care needs to be taken to make sure the best software -- with proper fields and correct information -- is in place or is going to be put in place.

The following are what we have seen to be important to address:

1. Alumni Organizational Committee

- It all begins with a group of leaders -- usually 5 - 10 alums -- who take an interest from the beginning. Many times these leaders come from those who have been involved in some manner in the school -- possibly through strategic planning, past fund-raising efforts, key donor work, etc. These people are crucial to future success because, as alums, they have got to set the pace.

2. Alumni Database

- This, as stated before, becomes the first focus area of action, after the alumni organizational committee is in place. All names, however old or inaccurate, must be plugged into the database.

3. Alumni Communication

- Communication is key. Many alums do not know what is going on at the school, and the only time they may have heard from you is to buy a raffle ticket or give money to the direct mail annual fund drive. The alumni newsletter, Facebook pages, e-mail blasts, and other means of communication are important to get the word out.
- With a direct mail newsletter, the school can put "ADDRESS CORRECTION REQUESTED" on the outside of the newsletter (by the mailing label) and some of those incorrect addresses will be corrected and sent back to the school. While you have to pay for it, this step becomes valuable in beginning to clean up the database.

4. "THE" Alumni Event

- One of the best ways to "rally the troops" when you are first beginning to organize the alums, is to have the alumni organizational committee sponsor (host) an event. This could be a homecoming, an anniversary, a reunion for a bunch of classes, or whatever.

5. Alumni Association

- One of the important decisions is whether you want to have an alumni association that all alums would belong to. This association could be "dues paying" or not. With an association, you could have bumper stickers and decals; you could try and get everyone to join; you could have guest speakers; you could coordinate in different geographic areas of the country. It has many possibilities.

6. Alumni Social Activities

- With input from the alumni organizational committee, and surveys to the alumni association and those attending THE event, you next need to poll the alum base to find out what they may be interested in and how often. Alumni softball tournament? Alumni basketball tournament? Alumni picnic? Alumni volleyball tournament? Alumni career day?

7. Alumni Reunions

- With an organized alumni effort, and an accurate database, the school should play a major role in the reunion efforts. In fact, working with class leaders, the school should be the one to initiate and help organize all reunions on a five-year cycle. The development office, acting as the catalyst, should do the following:
    - Help organize any five year reunion for that school year;
    - Motivate those classes who may not be thinking of a reunion to hold one -- with excellent support from the development office;
    - Provide class lists;
    - Publicize the reunions;
    - Help find lost alums;
    - Serve as the communication headquarters for the class;
    - Help schedule social events for the reunion;
    - Help organize a class mass, if applicable;
    - Meet on a regular basis with class leaders to help coordinate the reunion
    - Take pictures and write articles about the reunion;
    - Encourage classes to use the school facilities;
    - Invite "key" faculty members to the reunions.
- We strongly believe that Catholic schools could miss out on a wonderful opportunity to build relationships with alums if they take a passive role in the reunion process rather than an active role. Over and over, we see the value of serving as the "conductor" of these reunions by providing many of the items listed above. The main result that is reached with such an approach is the continuing development of the many gifts that alums have to offer.
- Some positive outcomes that we have seen take place:
    - Database gets put in shape.
    - Class leaders surface.
    - Alums reunite with their classmates and the school.

- ► Alums become interested in what is going on, presently, with the school.
- ► Alums start giving to the annual fund drive.
- ► Alum classes consider giving group gifts.
- ► Alums begin to step up and get involved in key areas of the school -- planning, *development*, career day, recruitment.
- ► Some alums begin to consider planned gifts to the school.
- ► The many gifts that alums have to offer get identified, and these alums are then invited to share those gifts of wisdom, of expertise, of finance, thereby becoming more engaged.

■ An alumni reunion weekend is an excellent event to schedule:

► Friday Night:	Social and open bar just with alums
► Saturday (day)	Games and tournaments
► Saturday (night)	Dinner and dance with spouses and/or “significant other”
► Sunday (morning)	Mass
► Sunday (noon)	Family picnic

■ Regardless of the plan or the activities, the development office should help coordinate every class reunion process.

8. Alumni Class Agents

■ Once the alumni effort gets on its feet, an organized class agent system would be great to put in place. Having 2-3 people responsible for each class, or block of classes, would allow the school to keep up with the database, keep track of lost alums, and communicate what is going on to all their former classmates.

9. Alumni E-mail

■ In the past 5-10 years, using e-mail addresses to stay in touch with alums is important. Always asking for e-mail addresses and keeping these addresses in an electronic file -- by class, by occupation, by whatever -- will prove to be very valuable in the future.

10. Alumni and Social Media

■ Although there are numerous social media vehicles in use today, we have found that there are three that Catholic schools are using with varying degrees of success with their alumni base:

- ► School Facebook page for constant posting by the school;
- ► LinkedIn connections by the school leaders to key alums;
- ► Twitter account for constant posting by the school.

As we know, using e-mail addresses to stay in touch with alums is important to the *development* efforts of all Catholic schools, and there is no better time to engage them than while they are still students in your school. So, before your students (elementary or high) graduate, go ahead and encourage them to do the following:

- Elect their alumni class officers and contact people.
- Induct them into the alumni association during one of the commencement exercises.
- Let them plan a one year reunion.
- Let them plan their five year reunion.
- Make sure all members of the graduation class have some kind of directory with every person's name, address, phone number, e-mail, name of next institution, etc.

It will be important for every Catholic school to continue to build the win-win relationships with its alumni base.

Lesson 19: Emphasize the Value and Use of Social Media.

According to my old marketing 101 textbook, the main focus of public relations and marketing was to spread the word about your products and services in order to get people to purchase. The 5 P's were the main words in order to describe the role of marketing: product, price, place, promotion, and packaging. I can remember using these words and how they apply to Catholic schools in a workshop I did for school principals about 15 years ago.

In their book, *Inbound Marketing*, Brian Halligan and Dharmesh Shah challenge us to think much differently. They cite several examples:

1. Five to ten years ago, buying large e-mail lists of "targeted names" and sending promotional materials worked well. Today, the National Canned Spam Act does limit what can be sent and to whom. And, according to Marketing Sherpa, the average open rate for an e-mail blast has gone down from 39% in 2004 to 18% in 2014.
2. Ten years ago, spending money on TV and radio was an excellent way to reach a large audience, but the addition of TiVo/DVRs to skip advertisements, the quantity of TV channels, the rise of video content online, and the emergence of XM/Sirius radio have dramatically lowered advertising's reach.
3. Ten years ago, letters, publications and newsletters were mailed out; today qualified people are blogging and publications are being sent and read online – especially if that business is able to get its web site linked to others.

Much like the concept of change processed in the book -- *Who Moved My Cheese?* -- are we ready to learn a whole new way of marketing and reaching people? Where are your alums communicating and finding information today? Where are the young alums -- the millennials -- who need to be reached by our Catholic schools? Where are the families that we need and want to attract to look at our Catholic schools? Where are the donors that Catholic school leaders want to reach? Where do our high school students gather information and communicate with each other?

According to Halligan and Shah, people "shop" and gather information in three main areas: 1. Through search engines such as Google; 2. Through blogosphere and its over 100 million blogs; 3. Through the social media sphere – Facebook, Twitter, LinkedIn, Digg, StumbleUpon, Reddit, YouTube and others. The ability to become known and effective all depends upon our ability to create *remarkable content.*

The authors believe that people visit websites because they are looking for something interesting that they can read and learn about. They offer three suggestions: 1. Add something collaborative to your website like a blog (which is updated on a regular basis); 2. Start creating lots of compelling content people will want to consume; 3. Start focusing on where the real action is: Google, industry blogs, and social media sites like Facebook, how-to articles for new Catholic parents and prospective school families, what-to-expect features for that pre-K family, short 2-3 minute videos of your students giving a testimonial on their Catholic school, interesting pictures of the dedication of your new science lab, blogs about your service program, new creative ideas you are implementing in technology, the latest information on how your graduates are doing as they are linked up to you on Facebook. These are all examples of how the world of communication and marketing continues to change how we operate.

Facebook is perhaps the largest and most active social networking site on the internet. It has millions of users who log on at least once per day, and the fastest growing demographic of people 35 years and older. As Halligan and Shah emphasize, what makes Facebook's reach particularly powerful is its viral aspect. When individual users join your school on Facebook, their friends see an update in their Facebook home page. This leads to more users joining your school's Facebook page, causing more people to be exposed to your Catholic school, and so on. By using this social aspect of Facebook, Catholic schools have the chance to reach large groups of people – quickly.

Getting started on Facebook is easy, but it will require ongoing attention in order to maintain its value, as users expect to see fresh information on your Facebook page. Once you are up and running, then the next obvious step is to start inviting people to be friends and fans. You can also link your Facebook page from your school web site and from other online materials so you can build within your community. However, you do want to be careful to set up your controls to invite people.

So, the rules have changed. According to David Meerman Scott, those who have grown up and continue to stick with the traditional marketing education that focused on the 5 P's, need to re-think. Those who have an MBA, or have trained on the job, have to unlearn and pick up some new skills. It is called *inbound marketing*, and the great news is that anybody can do it, and it does not require a lot of money, but it does require an investment of time and creativity. For those who don't think it works, be aware – regardless of your political preference – that this is what elected our latest president. Americans were able to connect with Obama via his blog, Facebook page (millions of supporters and counting), Twitter (over one million followers and counting), LinkedIn (thousands of members and counting), and YouTube (millions of views and counting) among other social networks and web sites.

Back when we started in Catholic school *development* in the mid-1980's, everything was all about building facilities with fiber optic cables; using technology to create databases; and sending out newsletters through direct mail. Ten years later in 1990's, it was all about laptops and websites; 10-12 years after that in 2009, it was all about setting up e-commerce; and, here it is in the middle of the second decade of the century and we have a major revolution that is staring us in the face. For all Catholic leaders, there is a place on this boat – in some kind of way. We hope, after doing your research and homework, you will be on board. There are all kinds of social media vehicles to use. For some of us, it has been a hard lesson to learn.

Lesson 20: Create a Culture of Giving.

Every Catholic school has a *culture of giving* – whether it is five years old, twenty-five years old, fifty years old, or just establishing itself in its community. We find that this *culture of giving* can alter and change and is usually established by the leaders in place (principal, pastor, president, board). Establishing this culture is not necessarily a conscious decision; many times it is "just the way we do things around here." It really applies to three areas: how a Catholic school invites the gifts, how it receives the gifts, and how the constituent base gives the gifts. All three – inviting, giving and receiving – go a long way in establishing that culture.

What is fascinating about this is that most Catholic schools have not really defined their *culture of giving*. "The way we've always done things" is usually the answer we receive when we probe on the question. With the present situation of Catholic schools throughout the country, there has never been a more important time than right now to define that giving culture. Eventually, with proper understanding, direction and process, a Catholic school can evolve into a *culture of giving* that will allow it to soar and prevail. The first step, however, is that we must understand the levels.

I would like to offer some language and levels that we could use to have us all understand what we mean by *culture of giving*. Let's consider the following four categories:

- Level 1: Little or No *culture of giving*
- Level 2: Basic *culture of giving*
- Level 3: Intermediate *culture of giving*
- Level 4: Advanced *culture of giving*

Once again, it is important to understand that this culture refers to inviting, giving, and receiving – all important in establishing the best culture for your Catholic school.

Let's talk about Level 1. Catholic schools at this level seem to function almost "hand to mouth." There is tuition, a fund-raiser or two or three or four or five, and maybe some subsidy. However, the parents, alums, parishioners, grandparents, past parents, and community have not been invited to become involved with the school – <u>in a meaningful way</u>. No one is really invited except maybe to buy a candy bar; giving is a second thought, and receiving is "catch as catch can." Sometimes at this level there is this "poor pitiful me Catholic syndrome" attitude that is working. "Please give to us because we are poor and cannot afford to do anything." There is little vision, unclear mission, no goals, no plans, and no processes in place to invite, involve and engage people. A *culture of giving* is hard to understand for those schools at Level 1. This can be summed up this way:

- Level 1 Inviting: Nothing personalized
- Level 1 Giving: Basic – what always has been done for years
- Level 1 Receiving: Little acknowledgement

Level 2 is interesting. Most schools who are at this level are either caught in the "same old, same old" mode or else they have taken the bull by the horns and are consciously climbing out of Level 1 into Level 2 and upward. Most schools at this level continue to deal with the 25-50-75 people who always do things at the school, and they have not opened up the doorways, avenues and roadways to engage people in a meaningful way. They still depend upon tuition, subsidy and some fund-raising events. Maybe some may be climbing up toward the next level, but advancing the school is all done by the principal and any volunteer help she/he can muster. No one is out in the community talking about the school and its features, its vision and its positive impact on that community. People are invited by direct mail or through a form letter or an e-mail; they give only the minimum in terms of prayer, service and financial contribution; and, the school receives the gifts as something "they" should be doing to keep the doors open. This is a very critical stage, because a Catholic school can only go up or down. And, if they are heading to the Level 1 category then the handwriting is on the wall as far as the future.

Level 2 can be summed up as follows:

- Level 2 Inviting: Quantity, not quality
- Level 2 Giving: Similar to Level 1 – what always has been done for years
- Level 2 Receiving: Some acknowledgement, appreciation and affirmation

With Level 3 – the Intermediate *culture of giv*ing – things begin to get exciting. Leaders don't feel sorry for themselves. There is bounce in their step, because there is a finite sense of direction. There is an active, well thought out process to invite, involve and engage people into the life of that Catholic school. Catholic schools at this level are not looking for a handout. They are interested in having a very clear mission, vision, and plan for the future. They create that plan through the engagement of people, and these same folks are the ones who help implement that plan and take it to the next level. Excitement is in the air, and benchmarks and progress can be seen. Principals take pride in their schools and talk about them at every turn of the road. School faculty and staff and administrators are on the same page. People are treated with courtesy and politeness when they register as a prospective family at the school. It is not the "same old, same old." People who do not have a sense of forward movement and positive attitudes are worked with, and if they do not get it, then the leaders work an exit process to help them find something else. Mediocrity is not tolerated; quality is strived for and attained in many areas. The school has made the conscious decision to devote the resources to putting the development office in place with the proper personnel. There is not a "gimme your money" tone that permeates. People are invited to share their gifts of prayer, service and financial participation. Development processes are in place to go beyond selling candy and holding a fair and festival or putting on an auction and dinner dance. Annual funds, capital campaigns, and some one-on-one work is being done. The leaders are consciously aware that parents, alums, parishioners, past parents, grandparents, the community, and others need to be constantly invited to be "stewards for a lifetime." In Level 3 we see the WIN-WIN attitude slowly begin to permeate the culture. It is not an "us vs. them" with teachers and students, or boards and parents, or school leaders and parents. This is an exciting level to reach. Let's sum it up this way:

- Level 3 Inviting: Moving more toward "eyeball to eyeball" invitation with creative processes for people to become engaged
- Level 3 Giving: People are giving their gifts – what they enjoy sharing with that Catholic school
- Level 3 Receiving: Excellent acknowledgement, appreciation and affirmation

Level 4 is the pinnacle, and yes, it is possible to stay there and keep getting better. The *culture of giving* at this level is outstanding. Unfortunately, there are not many Catholic schools that we have seen that are at this level, and there is one basic reason: They do not know their constituent base on a personal level, and they have not put the processes in place to develop the life-long relationships with them. At this level, parents and their families are met with each year – person to person – eyeball to eyeball. Either the pastor, the principal, the president, lead faculty members, board/council members, advancement/development officers, parent leaders, and others make it a point to meet with every family that makes up the parent base of that Catholic school. The *culture of giving* is established at the beginning of the relationship as these leaders cover four things in that annual conversation:

1. How are you doing?
2. Here is what we expect from you, and what do you expect from us?
3. What gifts would you enjoy sharing here in the school?
4. Is there anything we (as your child's school) can do for you and your family?

There is quality customer-service; there is a willingness to invite personally, give joyfully, and receive thankfully. This is established through building those relationships. Hundreds of people are invited and involved in strategic planning and in serving on boards and committees. There is room for everyone. Whatever gifts people have, they are invited to pray, discern, and decide what they wish to share – in terms of prayer, service and finance. Annual funds, capital campaigns, planned gifts, memorial gifts, endowment growth, and major gifts – these are all processes that grow out of this *culture of giving* at Level 4. People drive these processes.

By way of example, recently I attended the leadership reception of one of the high schools we are working with in the Midwest. The family who was hosting the reception has a beautiful home, and it was clear to see that the 80+ people in attendance were having a wonderful time. As the evening was drawing to a close, I had the opportunity to chat with the host and hostess. Now here was a couple who had graciously allowed the school to use their home, had paid for the catering, and had made a major gift to kick off this year's annual fund. They both stated to me that after their third child graduated this year, they were very interested in setting up a teacher endowment fund – to be used only for teacher professional advancement, and over the next xxx number of years they would be responsible for funding it on an annual basis. When I inquired further, they told me, "We came here not knowing anyone or anything, but very quickly we were personally invited and have served and used our resources to become partners with this school for a lifetime." As I was driving out of their driveway a little while later, I could only think: What a *culture of giving* they have established.

- Level 4 Inviting: Mostly personalized – one on one. School does not use the reasons of not enough time, not enough personnel, and not enough resources to make this happen. They make it happen because it is the very reason they are at Level 4.
- Level 4 Giving: People are creative in giving their gifts – what they enjoy sharing with that school
- Level 4 Receiving: Excellent acknowledgement, appreciation and affirmation

So, what is your *culture of giving*? It is so important to recognize, understand and address this. As Catholic institutions, our future depends upon it.

Lesson 21: Create the Written Strategic Plan for Development.

We realize that many Catholic schools have a development office of some kind in place. It may be a small operation; there may be a full time development director, or the effort could simply be something that school leaders are planning to get to in the future. Some of the reasons we have seen why *development* efforts begin have been referred to throughout this book and again listed here:

1. There is a strong need to bring in more money and so the development office is set up, a person hired, and the emphasis is on conducting fund-raising events, involving alumni, launching an annual fund, churning out a quarterly newsletter, building the database, or concentrating on strengthening the image so as to attract more students.
2. The school needs to hire someone who has experience, and that person will come in and "hit the ground running." Besides all of the above, the office will also concentrate on professional growth, possibly a capital campaign, engaging people, building an endowment, and setting up a planned giving effort.
3. The school has a strong need to launch a capital campaign to raise 7 or 8 figure money, and after going through that intensive process for 12 – 18 months, the establishment of a development office with a development director becomes a natural next step.

Obviously, there are other reasons, but these are the main ones we have seen since 1989.

Establishing the Infrastructure

As we have said, it is important that the *development* effort be set up to succeed. Some development "offices" open and there is no written plan of action, no general understanding by leaders (administration, school board, faculty and staff, parent leaders, alumni leaders, etc.) of what this *development* effort is supposed to accomplish, and little training for the person who is in charge of making it happen. In most cases, people just want to know, "How much money did you raise?"

Why not set up your *development* effort for the long term? Why go for the quick fix and have a development office that is nothing more than a glorified fund-raising program with event after event after event?

At the addendum of this book, there is a chart that we call the "Catholic School Development/ Advancement Infrastructure." (**See ISPD's Development/Advancement Infrastructure Chart**). Over the past 25+ years, we have taught this organizational chart to hundreds of Catholic institutions throughout the country, and many of these schools have made excellent strides, using this infrastructure as their foundation. Let us look closer.

At some point in time the "Catholic school leaders" (principal, pastor, board, etc.) makes the move to set up a "development office" with a "development officer". In the beginning years, the "development office" may be nothing more than a 4' x 8' table in the principal's office. And, the "development officer" may be a volunteer, the principal, or a teacher who works at it part-time. Please keep in mind that this chart's intention is to show how to "lay down the footprint for success."

The good signs are when the "leaders" have made their decision to begin a formal, organized effort; an "office" has been established, and an "officer" is in charge. It is then time to put in place

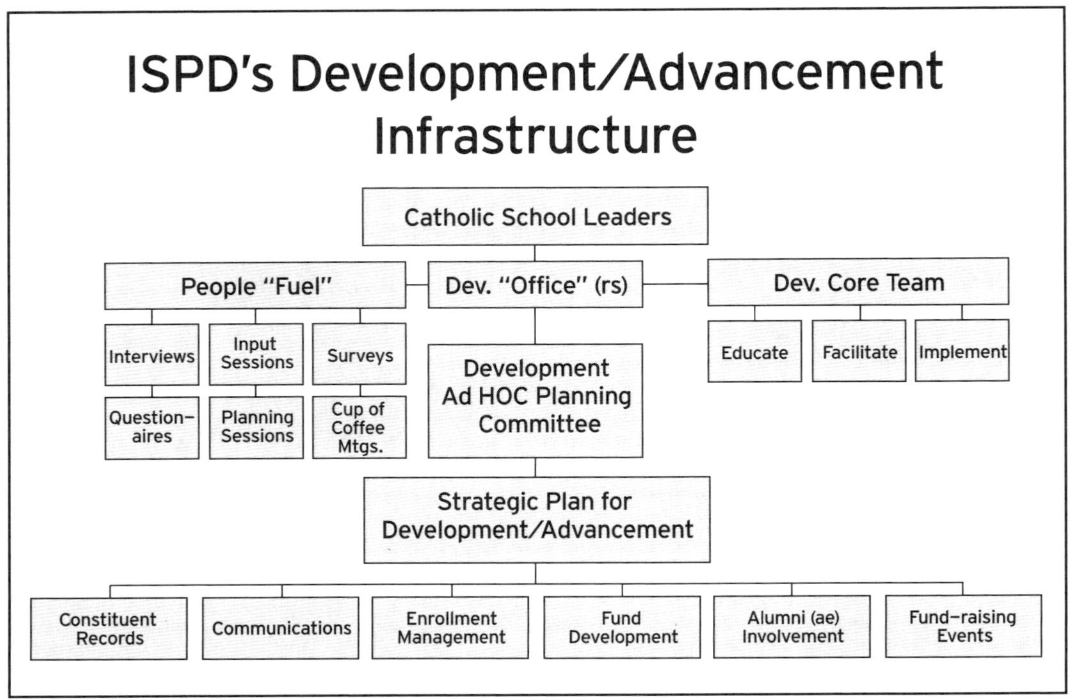

the most important group of people who will ever work with this effort – the "core team." As we have said earlier, this is a group of 15 – 18 people who are hand selected by the "school leaders" to work alongside the "development officer" in assuring that *development* is integrated into the life of the school. This "core team" is valuable, whether this is a new start or if your *development* "program" has been in place for years and years.

In the beginning months, the "core team" should concentrate on three items: 1. *Educating* all key leadership groups about what it plans to do and what Catholic school *development* is and is not; 2. *Facilitating* input and planning sessions; and 3. *Implementing* the priorities of the *strategic plan.*

While the "school leaders," the "core team," and the "officer" are getting this started, they need to make sure that they live by one rule: ***Invite and engage 100 uninvolved people into your Catholic school development effort each year***. These "uninvolved" people could be parents who have not stepped forward, alums who have not stayed in touch, parishioners who know nothing about the school, businesses in the community to whom you have never said hello. The list goes on and on. And, every bit of communication needs to have a personalized component to it.

You may be saying, "Invite them to what?" Listed on the chart, under "people fuel" are six input vehicles, all the way from interviews to input sessions to cup of coffee meetings. Please keep in mind that "people fuel" will be the key to future success. It will be the gas that will run your *development* engine. There are many, many ways to engage people into the life of a Catholic school.

Once you have the top three boxes under "Catholic School Leaders" in place ("development officer", "core team" and "people fuel"), you are ready to create the written *strategic plan for development*. How long does it take to put these first three boxes and their elements in place? Most

Catholic institutions accomplish this within 12 months; others take longer. However, please follow the compass and not the clock.

With the top of the chart in place, the next step is to personally invite approximately 75-100 people to be part of a four meeting process known as the "development ad hoc planning committee." (You can call this group whatever you wish). The *core team* will surface the names of the people, and we encourage that you use what we call the "60% - 40% rule." This suggests that 60% of the people you actually invite be uninvolved, and 40% of the people you invite be already engaged in the school in some capacity.

Once assembled, this large group is going to divide into smaller groups, and create action strategies under the six main planning areas that deal with Catholic school *development*. These planning areas are listed in this chart, and below there is a brief description of each.

- **Constituent Records**
    - We often say that your development efforts are only as good as your database. Pending on your needs, this could be an Excel spreadsheet, a database application like Access, software like File Maker Pro of ACT, or you may be using Raiser's Edge or e-Tapestry from Blackbaud. All of your Catholic school *development* efforts will find their base in your ***constituent records***.
- **Communication**
    - The ***communication*** area is where you develop your case statement and where you are able to articulate your mission and your vision. This is where you also develop your "WOW" which distinguishes you from other schools. The ***communication*** area of your *development* organizational structure can have many components:
        - Articulation and integration of your Catholic school's brand;
        - Publications such as newsletters and brochures and promotional materials;
        - Your website where you can visually display and articulate your messages;
        - Use of e-mail communication;
        - Use of social media;
        - The design elements of your communication efforts;
        - Use of media relations;
        - Photography of events and people.
- **Enrollment Management**
    - As we continue to emphasize, this is everyone's responsibility. Please notice that we have ***enrollment management*** as part of the overall *development* structure and not set off by itself and called admissions. With this area, Catholic schools manage their entire enrollment process – from attracting families to enrolling students to retaining those students. The ***enrollment management*** area depends and interacts with many areas of this organizational structure; the two we have already identified (***constituent records*** and ***communication***) are prime examples.

- **Fund Development**
  - ► By ***fund development***, we mean the annual fund, capital campaigns, major gift portfolios, endowments, planned giving and memorial giving. Out of all of these, the major one that most Catholic schools work with the most is the annual fund. This is the area that needs the most attention, because in many cases annual fund donors become capital campaign donors, and they can become planned giving and endowment donors. This area is a series of well-organized processes, and the annual fund stands out and needs the most attention and care.
- **Alumni(ae) Involvement**
  - ► As we all know, ***alumni(ae) involvement*** is so important to every Catholic school. The ability to bring back and involve your graduates – of all ages --- becomes the hidden gem to success. Whether you are an elementary school or a high school or a middle school or a Pre-K thru 12 school, this is an area that needs a lot of attention. In addition, this area interfaces with so many of the other areas we have mentioned thus far – namely ***constituent Records***, ***communications***, and ***fund development***.
- **Fund-Raising Events**
  - ► Unlike ***fund development***, ***fund-raising events*** is a "buy—sell" way of thinking. The Catholic school is looking to sell something – raffle tickets, raffle calendars, bingo cards and pull tabs, a chance to win a prize at the basketball booth, a ticket or sponsorship for the golf tournament, a car wash, ticket to the gala, and that list goes on and on. We recommend that ***fund-raising events*** do three things: 1. Raise good net dollars; 2. Build community; and, 3. Identify, promote and inspire leadership.
  - ► In terms of coordinating the ***fund-raising events*** and the processes in ***fund development***, we recommend the following flow of activities:
    - Annual fund (organized and comprehensive with chairs and divisions)
    - Three school-sponsored fund-raising events
    - Careful selection of other fund development process
      - On-going major donor portfolio work
        - ♦ Planned giving
        - ♦ Endowment growth
        - ♦ Tuition assistance
      - Capital campaign every 10 years

Now that we have given clarity to the six planning areas, let's move into the planning process.

The best way to do this is, before the planning sessions begin, the development office and the *core team* should create 1-2 Challenges under each of the six Planning Areas. For example, under ***enrollment management*** the challenge may be: "How can we build stronger relationships with our partner/feeder school principals and pastors?" Under ***alumni(ae) involvement*** the challenge may be: "How can we reach out to our out of state alums and better communicate the many exciting things going on here at our Catholic school?" Or, "How can we create and organized an annual homecoming for our elementary school alumni that will be fun, exciting, and meaningful?"

Working through four meetings, and dividing into 4-5 small groups, the "development ad hoc planning committee" will be asked to *solve the challenges* with creative strategic initiatives – all beginning with action verbs. Through problem solving, this group of people will actually create the draft, written *strategic plan for development*. You will then have the plan to move your development efforts forward. What you will also find is that over 40% of the people who work with you in this effort will also stay on to help you implement the Plan. And yet, at the heart of it all are the "development office" and the "core team." They assure continuity, consistency and reality.

The SPD ("strategic plan for development"), once prioritized, is usually "good to go" for 12-18 months, and then it will need to be revisited. When you revisit it, you will need to affirm the accomplishments, explore new challenges in the six planning areas, create new strategic initiatives, and set the plan up for the next 12-18 months. In addition, you will need to invite 25-30 people from the first planning committee, and the other 50-60 need to be new and uninvolved. By keeping the plan refreshed, you also keep your efforts relevant, and most importantly, you keep people meaningfully involved, which is the heart and soul of a Catholic *development* effort.

Lesson 22: Implement the Proper Preparation and Organization for a Capital Campaign.

The launching of a capital campaign in a Catholic school is a major undertaking – one that requires months and months of planning, and sometimes years of nuancing in order to make sure the school is ready to kick off a campaign that will be successful. What level your *culture of giving* is at is also something to consider.

Tongue in cheek, we have often said that a Catholic school capital campaign is the Super Bowl, the Final Four, the Stanley Cup, the NBA Finals, the Master's Golf Tournament – using all of those sports analogies. It is so important to be ready.

Catholic schools usually launch capital campaigns in order to raise 7-8 figure money to build new buildings, renovate old ones, establish endowments in various areas, and set the tone for a new vision for the next 5-10 years.

We have always taught that there are five phases to a capital campaign:

- Phase 1: Exploration – Discovery – Feasibility
- Phase 2: Campaign Organization
- Phase 3: Pacesetter (Silent) Phase
- Phase 4: Public Phase
- Phase 5: Operation Homestretch!

With these phases in mind, there are key steps we have learned over the years that can serve as wonderful lessons to move your Catholic school forward in a capital campaign. We would like to present those steps in this lesson.

The Feasibility Phase

1. Form the *steering committee* that will guide the campaign process from beginning to end.
2. Have the school leaders establish the major threads (short term/long term) they want to present to school's stakeholders. (These are often referred to as the case points). These major threads are what the school would be raising the money for.
3. Once the draft list of these major threads is decided, seek input from the various constituents that make up the school.
4. Make sure the necessary demographic data will support any future site master plan and the campaign.
5. Finalize the case points for a possible capital campaign.
6. Create, publish and distribute a Q&A booklet that asks and answers pertinent questions about an upcoming campaign.
7. If applicable, conduct a survey (usually through input/listening sessions) in regards to the order of importance of the major threads.

8. Create the case statement and/or the position statement for a possible campaign.
9. Have outside counsel conduct the financial feasibility study by interviewing the top 50+ potential donors for a campaign.
10. Make the recommendation to move forward or not. If yes, then move to campaign organization.
11. Get necessary approvals.
    - Board/Council
    - Diocese

The Campaign Organization Phase

12. Set up the campaign organization and recruit key positions.
    - Operational and honorary (if applicable)
    - Pacesetter chairs: special, lead, major and leadership divisions
    - Public chairs: parent and alumni divisions
    - Public chairs: friends and business community divisions
    - New parent gift division chairs
13. Clean up database with key information for the campaign.
14. Continually educate the key campaign leaders on their focus in the campaign
    - Operational Chairs
        - Recruit division leaders
        - Share wisdom in key areas
        - Organize and focus the Campaign
        - Help plan pacesetter phase
        - Help plan public phase
        - Secure gifts from campaign leaders
    - Honorary:
        - Lend name to the campaign
        - Attend pacesetter reception
        - Support financially
        - Invite 1-3 people to participate financially
    - Pacesetter Chairs:
        - Recruit teams
            - Lead: Gold Medal Committee
            - Major: Blue Ribbon Committee

        - Leadership: captains
    - ► Get team members to the training
    - ► Offer your best wisdom on key issues of the Campaign
    - ► Help plan pacesetter reception
    - ► Attend receptions
    - ► Keep communication wide-open up and down the lines
- ■ Public Phase: Parents/Alumni
    - ► Recruit teams
    - ► Offer your best wisdom on key issues
    - ► Attend pacesetter reception
    - ► Invite $$$ gift from team members
    - ► Help organize public phase kick-off event
    - ► Coordinate and attend receptions when possible
    - ► Maintain on-line accounting
- ■ Public Phase Chairs: Friends (past parents, grandparents, friends)
    - ► Seek gifts from school's past parents
    - ► Decide what role grandparents will serve
    - ► Build database
- ■ Public Phase Chairs: Business Community
    - ► Create case for support
    - ► Identify businesses
    - ► Select captains
    - ► Establish "connectors"
    - ► Train division chairs and captains

15. Campaign leaders need to address key issues to the Campaign:
    - ■ Money ranges suggested
    - ■ Gift giving divisions
    - ■ Naming opportunities
    - ■ Campaign materials
    - ■ *Update* Bulletins
    - ■ Campaign Messages

16. Establish Campaign Office.
    - Development personnel
    - Physical location
17. Recruit teams for lead, major, leadership, parent, alumni, friends and business community.
18. Train all people in the pacesetter divisions.
19. Create and finalize all campaign materials.
    - Campaign prayer
    - Pocket folder
    - Case statement/brochure
    - Video
    - Letter of intent (LOI)
    - Q & A
    - Fact sheet
    - Campaign pyramid
    - Payment breakdown sheet
    - Campaign stationery
20. Set up and implement campaign accounting and communication.
21. Secure campaign leaders' LOIs (Letters of Intent) before pacesetter reception.
    - Steering committee
    - Op chairs
    - Honorary chairs
    - Division leaders
    - Gold medal committee
    - Blue ribbon committee
    - Leadership captains

The Pacesetter Phase

22. Host pacesetter reception.
23. Invite and secure pacesetter LOIs.

The Public Phase

24. Organize public gift divisions.
25. Train teams in public gift division.

- Parent: grade level chairs and class captains
- Alumni: decade chairs and class reps
- Friends: division chairs
- Business Community: captains

26. Implement the Public Gift Divisions.
    - Public kick off
    - Home receptions
    - Public receptions
    - One-on-one visits
    - Out of town visits
27. Complete all visits in all divisions.

The Operation Homestretch Phase

28. Organize and implement wrap-up phase.
29. Celebrate success.
30. Phase back into vibrant *advancement* efforts.

Another way of looking at a capital campaign is through the lens of a visual we created a number of years ago. We call it the Traffic Light Process for a capital campaign. (***See ISPD's Traffic Light Process Chart***). The premise behind this process is that you do not proceed to the next light until the one on which you are working turns green. This is another way of preparing and implementing.

Indeed, there are multiple steps to be taken in a capital campaign. There is a lot more involved than simply taking the number of parents and alums that make up the database of a Catholic school and dividing that number into the amount of money that you are trying to raise. How many times have we heard Catholic school leaders say, "Well we need to raise $3,000,000. Combined, we have 3,000 alums and parents, so if everyone gave $1,000 then we would reach our goal." We wish it were that simple. Through experience, we have found that many (not all) capital campaigns work by the rule of one-thirds:

- The first 1/3 of the money comes from 5-10 key donors.
- The second 1/3 of the money comes from the next 100-200 donors.
- The final 1/3 of the money comes from everyone else.

As we have said in this lesson, it is important to set up the right preparation and organization in order to be successful. You do want to win that Super Bowl.

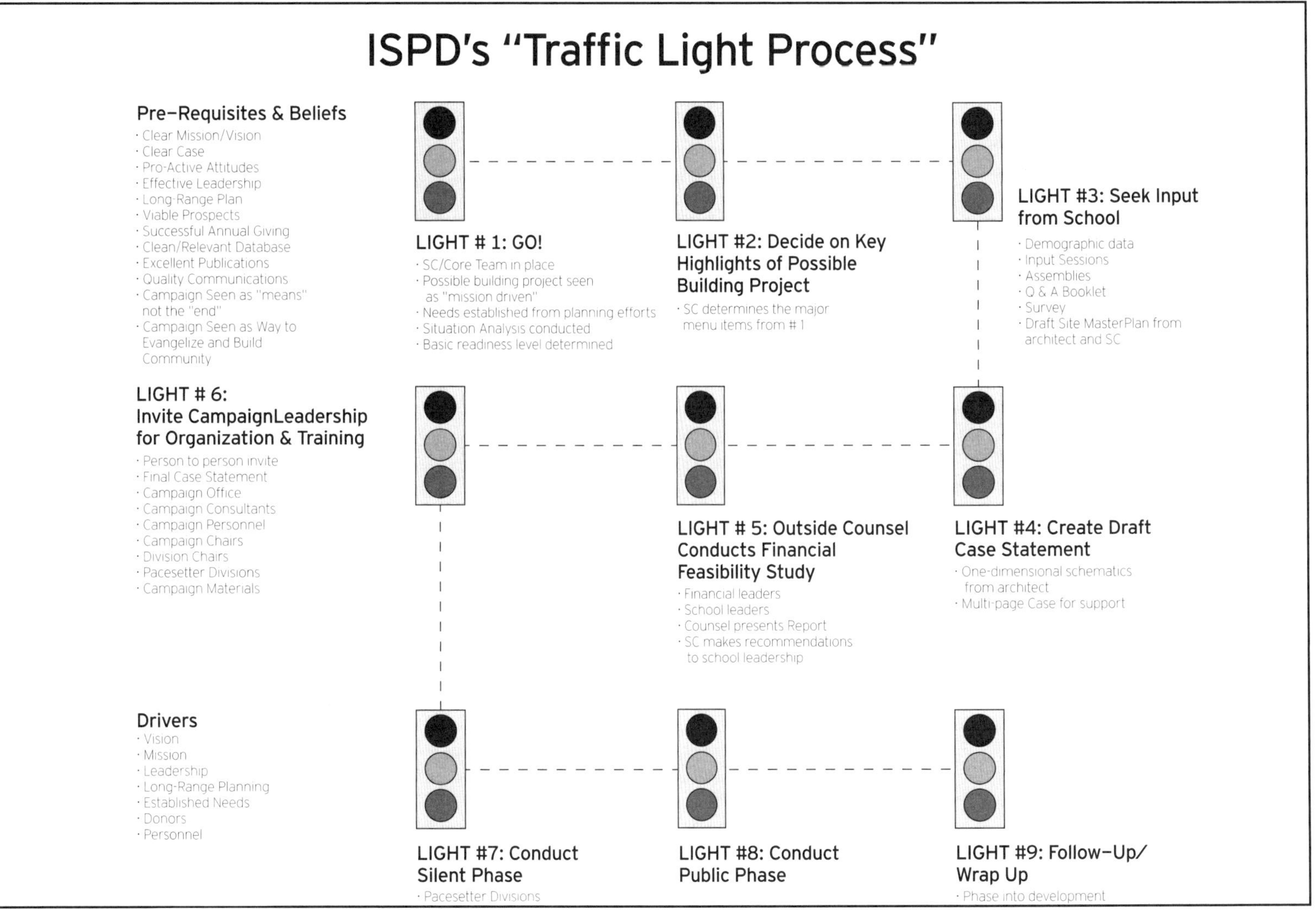
ISPD's "Traffic Light Process"
Pre–Requisites & Beliefs
· Clear Mission/Vision
· Clear Case
· Pro-Active Attitudes
· Effective Leadership
· Long-Range Plan
· Viable Prospects
· Successful Annual Giving
· Clean/Relevant Database
· Excellent Publications
· Quality Communications
· Campaign Seen as "means" not the "end"
· Campaign Seen as Way to Evangelize and Build Community
LIGHT # 1: GO!
· SC/Core Team in place
· Possible building project seen as "mission driven"
· Needs established from planning efforts
· Situation Analysis conducted
· Basic readiness level determined
LIGHT #2: Decide on Key Highlights of Possible Building Project
· SC determines the major menu items from # 1
LIGHT #3: Seek Input from School
· Demographic data
· Input Sessions
· Assemblies
· Q & A Booklet
· Survey
· Draft Site MasterPlan from architect and SC
LIGHT # 6: Invite CampaignLeadership for Organization & Training
· Person to person invite
· Final Case Statement
· Campaign Office
· Campaign Consultants
· Campaign Personnel
· Campaign Chairs
· Division Chairs
· Pacesetter Divisions
· Campaign Materials
LIGHT # 5: Outside Counsel Conducts Financial Feasibility Study
· Financial leaders
· School leaders
· Counsel presents Report
· SC makes recommendations to school leadership
LIGHT #4: Create Draft Case Statement
· One-dimensional schematics from architect
· Multi-page Case for support
Drivers
· Vision
· Mission
· Leadership
· Long-Range Planning
· Established Needs
· Donors
· Personnel
LIGHT #7: Conduct Silent Phase
· Pacesetter Divisions
LIGHT #8: Conduct Public Phase
LIGHT #9: Follow–Up/ Wrap Up
· Phase into development

Lesson 23: Fuel Endowment Growth with Planned and Capital Gifts.

When I first became involved in Catholic school *development*, growing the endowment was top priority. In fact in the late 1990's this was seen as important as implementing an annual fund. The reasons for endowment growth are obvious. However, over the past 10-15 years we have seen a change in thinking. There are not that many Catholic schools who want their money sitting in an endowment fund with the market as volatile as it has been in past years. We are not denying that endowment growth is important, but we see more and more Catholic schools creating various ways to fund endowments rather than launching an endowment campaign all by itself. Here are ways we have observed:

1. Fund endowment through a percentage of a capital campaign.
2. Fund endowment as one of the case points of a capital campaign. For example, in a recent $6,000,000 campaign, school leaders wanted to designate $1,000,000 as an endowment for tuition assistance.
3. Fund endowment through planned giving growth.
4. Although not that effective, some schools try and fund endowments through a percentage of the annual fund, a percentage of a major school fund-raiser, or a special fund raiser specifically targeted to the endowment.

One major lesson we have learned is that it is important to establish a process to seek and receive planned gifts. This is where most of the endowment growth is going to happen. We would like to share with the reader, as part of this section on *Processes and Structures to Advance Catholic Schools* the steps to set up a vibrant planned giving effort.

Step One: Establish the Planned Giving Council.

When a Catholic school makes the decision to move into planned giving, it will need a group of people to "get the ball rolling." What you need here are leaders, communicators, and individuals who are not afraid of visiting people and offering opportunities. Members of this council should come from the board, parents, alumni leaders, past parents, etc. We like to see this group number between 8-12 persons, not including *development* personnel. This group should not be the "experts."

Step Two: Set up the Planned Giving "Office" and "Officer."

It will be important to establish a physical location in the school where planned giving records are kept, literature is displayed, a phone rings, a fax receives, and prospective donors and members of the planned giving council have a person with whom they can speak. It will also be important to have one person designated as the "planned giving officer." This person will be responsible for the process and its implementation.

Step Three: Secure a Tax Attorney and/or CPA.

One of the main reasons Catholic schools do not pursue planned giving is because they are intimidated by it. That is natural. However, offering opportunities is what the council and the development officers can do. Let the tax attorneys work out the details. Many schools have found tax attorneys who were willing to donate their time and expertise to set up various planned giving vehicles -- pending a request from the donor. Oftentimes, the school's tax attorney and the donor's tax attorney can work out the details without the school being involved at all. Also, many dioceses have excellent resource people who can handle all of the particulars of a detailed planned gift.

Step Four: Establish the Philosophy and Rationale of Planned Giving.

One of the first tasks the planned giving council should take on is to establish the philosophy and rationale on why the school is setting up the planned giving efforts. A strong case should be made on why this is important, and how this differs from other forms of giving.

Step Five: Create the Mission Statement.

The planned giving council should create a mission statement explaining the purpose. This, obviously, will draw from the philosophy and rationale discussions. 1-2 sentences is all that is needed here for the mission.

Step Six: Establish Goals and Strategies.

It will be important to establish first year goals and objectives. Goals should be viewed as giving "direction." Strategies should be viewed as the action plan that will allow the goals to be accomplished. For example:

- Direction: To determine donor attitudes on planned giving
- Strategy: Conduct interviews with the top 20 donor prospects in order to determine their attitudes, wishes, and interests.

Step Seven: Create the Investment Policies and Guidelines.

Each planned giving effort has its own policies and guidelines. Sometimes these are established by the diocese and/or the school. It will be important to establish these policies and guidelines from the very beginning. These should be created by the planned giving council and approved by the principal and/or pastor.

Step Eight: Identify the Top Donor Prospects.

The identification and cultivation of donors is an on-going process and should be one of the main functions of the planned giving council. Council members, along with the development officers, need to be trained in donor research and identification. Although it may be difficult to identify many people right away, the council and the officers should begin with some "raw" list based upon past giving history. At least 25+ should be identified. Many of these will come from the donor lists of a capital campaign, the annual fund, the foundation, etc.

Step Nine: Begin the Donor Cultivation Process.

Working with donors who may make a planned gift is a long process. This is not an overnight activity. It will be very important, with the initial donor ID, for the council and development officers to begin an organized cultivation process. All need to be trained in cultivation, as these people who have been identified -- in some cases -- have very little connection to the school. Constant education and personal relationships will be the key.

Step Ten: Have Council and Officers Receive Necessary Training.

It will be important to establish an on-going training and educational component of the planned giving process. As stated earlier, schools that succeed in all of this will be the ones who treat their staff and volunteers with the utmost respect and offer the best in training. It cannot be assumed that everyone on a planned giving council would know how to visit and invite.

Step Eleven: Have a Conversation with the Top 20+ Donors.

One of the first things a Catholic school will do is create literature without first asking, "What does the customer need?" We strongly recommend that the planned giving council, after the establishment of the first ten steps, conduct one-on-one visits with the top 20+ donor prospects. The purpose of these visits is threefold:

1. Establish the beginning of a relationship;
2. Find out how the donor feels about the school;
3. Explain that the school is starting a planned giving process, and one of the main purposes of the visit is to "ask the customer" what his/her/their needs are.

Step Twelve: Identify the Key Planned Giving Opportunities to Offer in the Literature.

After the interviews, the planned giving council should decide on the key opportunities that they would like to concentrate on. These will be the main items that will be featured in the literature. With so many different kinds of planned giving "vehicles," it is easy to get confused and have the donor not even know what to look for. The interviews should provide some excellent information:

- What kind of opportunities are most popular;
- Attitudes about the school;
- Possible identification of other planned giving donors, as the visitor asks, as one of the final questions, "Bob, is there anyone you know whose input and ideas you feel we need to get on this whole planned giving process?"

Step Thirteen: Create the Literature and Public Relations Pieces.

Now that the council knows what the customer needs, it will be important to create the necessary literature. Two types of pieces should be considered: 1. A "stand alone" brochure that can be used all the time; 2. Regular mailings (possibly newsletters) that can be used on a consistent basis -- each with different messages. The key pieces we see as being effective are:

- Planned giving brochure
- Planned giving newsletter (2x's -- 4x's per year)
- Planned giving video

Step Fourteen: Invite People onto Your Campus.

It will be important to invite people to come to the campus for some kind of event. Possibly, the council can offer an educational workshop on charitable remainder trusts, or some kind of presentation on new tax laws -- federal and state, and how they impact inheritance. This will produce a pool of "prospects." It will also be important in the interviews to see what kind of presentations, seminars, workshops, etc. people would like to attend.

Step Fifteen: Continue the On-going Research and Nurturing.

Catholic *development* is all about people -- not just dollars. It is imperative for the council and the development officers to continue to research and visit people -- all the time. This is not a one-time effort. It will not be enough to see a key donor once every two years. An on-going relationship must be established.

Planned giving is key to the future of Catholic schools. However, it is not a quick fix. A donor must feel good about the school and its mission, leadership and WOW!. It will be important for the development officers and the council to concentrate on the people component, and let the tax experts handle the details. Relationships will be the key to success; it will take time to build a vibrant plan.

Lesson 24: Be Open to Change and Shifts in Thinking.

There is a passage from *Boy's Life* by Robert McCammon that I often use in workshops and also in working with clients. Actually, it is the opening chapter of the novel in which the author talks about change and creativity and being able to remember the "wildness" of our youth when we were alive and free and saw the world through the eyes of a dreamer. It is a wonderful piece that challenges us to realize that maybe, just maybe, we need to do things differently, and that the greatest challenges we face are mediocrity and always approaching situations the same way time after time after time.

There is another passage that I have always liked: *The answers and the solutions that we used to get us to where we are today will not be the same answers and solutions that will get us where we want to be tomorrow.*

We find that some Catholic schools have been doing the same things over and over and still expect the results to be different. For example, I was visiting a Catholic high school a little over a year ago. They had asked me to come in and give a talk to their board on what "customer service" meant in a Catholic high school. While waiting for the business of the meeting to be completed, I sat there rather stunned when the chair of the board stated that they were planning to increase the dollar goal of the annual fund by 20% the next year. Now, here it was in March; the goal was already $150,000 for that year, and they had generated a little over $70,000 and were not expecting more than another $35,000 to come in to the school. So, if the annual fund ended up reaching $105,000 in that year ($45,000 short), what in the world was going to make it increase by 20% the following year? When I asked that question at the board meeting and there was no answer, I knew right away that my question was not something they wanted to entertain. The bottom line was: They needed more money. How would it be gotten? I don't know if they had that answer.

Now, are there ways to increase an annual fund and grow it over a period of years? Definitely. However, the "people base" must increase for that to happen, and the retention of donors needs to be high. Many Catholic schools need to invest the time and the effort to engage people in a meaningful manner. That is the main shift we encourage all to make.

I call it "shifts in thinking" because that usually is what it takes for a Catholic school to go through positive change. The climate must be right; the leadership must be educated and receptive; and, there must be a positive plan of action to make something happen. Out of all of the lessons we are discussing in this book, this one goes to the heart of making something happen – are we willing to change?

Here are five "shifts" that we encourage Catholic schools to think about and questions we invite all to answer:

- **Lead buffalo of the herd or a gaggle of geese who share responsibility?**
    - Are your *development* efforts moving forward with a T-E-A-M effort or with "boss management" as the norm?
    - Are the people making the decisions inviting input from those working in the area of *development*?

- ▶ Do the leaders of your Catholic school really understand *development,* and are they willing to *develop* for the future by inviting, involving and engaging people?
- ▶ Are changes in *development* goals researched or just *knee-jerk* reactions to deficient budgets?
- ▶ Are you spending at least 25% of your *development* time building relationships with people?

■ **Willing to invest and cultivate or just interested in short-term results?**

- ▶ Are the leaders of your Catholic school willing to invest in the future or is crisis-management the norm?
- ▶ Are the attitudes of your leaders more reactive or more proactive?
- ▶ Do those working in *development* look for WIN-WIN situations?

■ **Process rather than program thinking?**

- ▶ Are your *development* efforts centered around one *program* after another (golf tournament, raffle calendar, auction and dinner dance, bingo, Christmas tree sale, quarterly newsletter, etc.) or is there constant improvement through the use of processes year to year that form a *development system*?
- ▶ Do the *development* leaders understand and follow the 7 "I" process of *Identify – Inform – Invite – Involve – Implement – Invest – Improve*?

■ **Building genuine relationships with people or just going after the money?**

- ▶ Are the leaders of your Catholic school all about building relationships or do they get to know people because those people have financial means?
- ▶ Are you inviting people to become involved in your Catholic school because you really value their expertise, talent, and wisdom or because you feel if you involve them they will give you money?

■ **Change as a natural process or change as a crisis?**

- ▶ Do your Catholic leaders understand that real change usually does not take place without challenges?
- ▶ Do your leaders realize that good positive change can come from these challenges?
- ▶ Do your leaders know the percentages of people and their reactions to change?
    - • 8% are usually the *innovators* who create the new ideas and then lead the change.
    - • 17% are the *leaders* who are open to change once it has been introduced to them.
    - • 29% are the *early majority* who are usually the followers once they have been convinced.
    - • • 29% are the *late majority*, and they are usually very skeptical and may not change at all.

- 17% are the *destroyers* who are usually adamant about change taking place and who are usually willing to make sure they destroy any new ideas or thoughts. Usually, the new creativity or new process is a threat to their *guarded kingdom*.

Innovation and creativity usually come by inviting new people into the Catholic school *development* system. Cultural change is not easy, but shifts in thinking are vital if we are going to keep our Catholic schools alive and prosperous. Years from now, what will be said about the leadership in our time? Who will the shapers have been? Who will make sure our Catholic schools remain open and vibrant?

It is not the critic who counts.

Not the one who points out how the weak one stumbled

Or the doer of deeds could have done them better.

The credit belongs to the one who is actually in the arena,

Whose face is marred with toil and sweat and blood,

Who errs and yet comes back time and time again,

Who knows the great sweetness of victory and the bitterness of defeat.

And, in the end if that person falls short,

At least it is done daringly,

So that his soul may never be cast with those cold and timid ones

Who sit on the sideline, complain, and point fingers,

And never even know defeat nor victory itself.

(Paraphrased from Teddy Roosevelt)

Lesson 25: Explore New Sources of Revenue with a Proactive Stance.

For the past fifteen years we have stated the following, "The age-old model of trying to fund Catholic schools with tuition, subsidy, and fund-raisers is obsolete, ineffective and will cease to sustain our schools in the future."

We have gone on to say, "We must stop the downward spiral of raising tuition when the budget does not balance, or telling the development office to increase the annual fund with no strategies on how to make that happen, or adding more fund-raisers, or freezing teachers' salaries, or cutting out needed programs because they will throw off the budget."

We have offered seven suggestions that we referred to as Level One Focus:

1. Catholic school leaders need to make a decision: either fully support Catholic schools and make them work using every possible resource or let the strong survive.
2. Encourage Catholic leaders to convene congresses, convocations, think-tanks in order to bring people together to solve the challenges we face in funding Catholic schools.
3. Make sure that Catholic schools are outstanding in all areas.
4. Catholic schools must build strong faith communities: the network that is touched by the mission of that Catholic school.
5. Catholic school leaders must engage every single Catholic family by personally interacting with them and understanding their needs, their gifts, their capabilities, and ways they wish to be involved.
6. Finance councils must explore new frontiers.
7. All parishioners must be continually invited to witness the true value of a Catholic school and come to understand how Catholic schools are the greatest evangelizers of the Catholic faith to young people on a daily basis.

With that said, we now move to what we call "Level Two Focus": What are specific funding strategies that could vastly improve this age old model?

We view this approach very much like a menu of options. When my family goes into a cafeteria or attends a pot luck at the school, we may not all like the same offerings; some appeal more to me than to my wife or to my daughter. Same thing here. Because of a Catholic school's history, culture, location, position in the community, budget demands, debt service, etc., each school will be different in terms of what will work and what can be tried.

That said, we believe that there are four sources that are equally responsible for the funding of Catholic schools – the family, the school, the parish and the diocese. With the age old model, the family is responsible for the following: paying tuition; paying fees; and supporting the fund-raisers. The school receives the tuition, gets a subsidy of some kind (parish and/or state – possibly), runs the fundraising events and organizes the *development* efforts. Many parishes subsidize their schools

-- some with over 50% of their parish budget, and some (yet few) dioceses fund with investment income from an endowment for Catholic schools. All of this varies from diocese to diocese and even from deanery to deanery and school/parish to school/parish.

We believe we must open wide the doors to new opportunities. We must call all Catholic leaders together, knock down some guarded kingdoms, and realize there are options, menus, choices, and chances that must be taken in order for Catholic schools to survive.

There is no silver bullet. We wish we could say that there was, but as one principal said recently, "You know, cost-based/needs-based tuition worked great in this neighboring diocese, but in our area, people hated it, so we just tabled it for now." That is why it is so important to view the full menu, to realize that some of these items are new and will require a leap of faith. One thing we do know is what we have said for years, "The solutions that have gotten us to where we are today will not be the same solutions that will get us to where we want to be tomorrow."

Let's look at each area and list the possibilities or the options of opportunities. With the four sources, there are a lot of crossover areas, and that is understandable. Please understand that these are suggestions with other options and creative solutions yet to be explored.

1. The Family

- Continue with the traditional model of tuition, fees and supporting fund-raisers. This will be open for those families who can afford to attend that Catholic school.
- Open the Catholic school to every Catholic family who wants to receive a Catholic education. Enter into a true partnership between the school and the family through one-on-one conversations and visits and determine what is feasible in terms of what gifts that family can bring/afford:
    - Gifts in kind
    - Gifts of professional service
    - Amount of money that can be afforded for that child or those children's education
    - Money they can raise through their own fund-raising efforts, after being educated on how to generate funds through workshops sponsored by the school
    - Needs-based/cost-based tuition
    - Money that can be generated with student working for and with a school approved business

2. The School

- Generate money through tuition, subsidy and fund-raising events.
- Put in place a vibrant *development/advancement* effort that will concentrate on:
    - Annual fund
    - Capital campaign

- ► Endowment growth
- ► Planned gifts
- ► Memorial giving
- ► Major gifts

- ■ Educate and promote needs-based/cost-based tuition.
- ■ Explore business and corporate partnerships.
- ■ Explore retail sales within the school.

3. The Parish

- ■ Offer subsidy to the Catholic school(s) based upon the number of students attending from that parish.
- ■ Move to the total stewardship model where Catholic schools are made available for every Catholic family based upon the gifts (prayer, service, finance) that the family offers to the parish. All gifts will have benchmarks that must be agreed upon by the family, the school and the parish. (Diocese of Wichita model).

4. The Diocese

- ■ Study and, if available and feasible, offer vouchers for families.
- ■ Continue to understand, research and make available state and/or federal subsidies grants and vouchers.
- ■ Launch a diocesan-wide capital campaign to build an endowment fund for Catholic schools (Diocese of Fort Wayne/South Bend) and fund every year.
- ■ Research and consider charter-type schools with diocesan affiliation.
- ■ Establish a Catholic school foundation (Seeds of Hope in Archdiocese of Denver) that will raise money every year to fund Catholic schools.
- ■ Explore the financial value of new governance through systems, collaboration and/or regionalization.

These are all options, and there is no "one size fits all." But, these opportunities do provide different ways of looking at the available resources and revenues for Catholic schools. Now, the reader can hopefully see the value of Catholic leaders convening congresses and convocations in order to introduce these options (and more) and discuss new solutions to age old challenges. We do have many opportunities if we will only break down the barriers of mediocrity and explore. Now is the time to call people together – in all four entities – and make some very important decisions.

SECTION D: PARTING THOUGHTS

Since Hurricane Katrina, my wife and daughter and I have been living out in the country on a 25 acre piece of land that has been in our family since the 1940's. It is where I grew up, and where I eventually returned. It is a beautiful piece of property right in the heart of south Louisiana close to the Mississippi state line. In August 2005, when the hurricane destroyed much of our home near Lake Pontchartrain, we made the decision to go ahead and speed up the building plans we had for the future and build a log home on the property my dad and mom had left to me and my brother. It is 15 miles north of where we used to live, very high ground, and not in a flood zone. After living in a little 600 square foot guest house (that had been on the property since 1961) for two years after Katrina while this house was being built, we finally moved in to our new home in July 2007.

Being right on Morgan's River, which runs into the Pearl River about ½ mile down from us, we are blessed with wonderful fishing, bird watching, and the ability to walk out of our back door and see wood ducks swimming with their young as they paddle down the bayou. I thank God every day for the foresight my parents had in finding and buying this property -- which back in 1942, sold for $400.00 per acre.

One of the mainstays of the farm has always been the one acre garden that my dad used to manage and take care of until he passed away in 2003 at the ripe old age of 98. For years and years, that garden provided some of the best meals we ever ate. During the summer time, we never ran out of sweet corn, tomatoes, cucumbers, pole beans, field peas, squash, okra, peppers, cantaloupes, and watermelons. In the fall and winter, we always had plenty of lettuce, mustard greens, collard greens, turnip greens, potatoes, broccoli, cauliflower, carrots, and swiss chard. The spring garden was filled with the same; it was a year round venture.

I was lucky to learn the little I do know from my dad; he had the green thumb, even up to making sure we harvested our own honey from the bee hives he kept around the property -- making sure the bees pollinated the many vegetable flowers growing in the garden. It was a wonderful learning experience growing up with a father who had an intense love of the land and the ability to grow almost anything that the climate of south Louisiana could produce.

Although he probably did not think I was paying any attention at all, I observed the many, many hours he spent *developing* his garden - day by day, week by week, month by month, and year by year. This was not a *program* where one year he said, "Let's grow some G-90 sweet corn." No, this was a process that started early on in his life -- a keen recognition that in order to be successful he had to identify the best crops to grow in this climate, make sure the soil was tested for the proper chemical balance, and then, based upon those results, prepare that soil with the best fertilizers for that environment. He had to cultivate the ground and then till it up. Afterwards, he had to organize his garden and decide where everything would go. He had to set up the rows and know how high each one needed to be. He had to know when to plant each crop, whether or not to start that crop inside in a seed bed or go ahead and plant it straight into the ground. He had to know how far to space the seeds in a row, and which vegetables did best when grown together or next to each other. Once in the ground, the work was just beginning, because being an organic gardener, he did not use pesticides or anything poisonous. He had to watch each crop daily and make adjustments with the right kind of organic dust to rid the plants of dangerous insects. He had to nurture everything he planted, making sure to hoe away all of the grass and weeds and be quick to pick any foreign bugs off of the leaves. With certain crops, he needed to know when to pick them and when they were ready. With some - like broccoli, squash, okra, and greens -- picking them at the right time allowed for further development and more of the same.

After many of the crops had run their course, dad would always make sure that he saved some of the seeds, dried them out, and got them ready for use for the next year. Many of the vegetables perpetuated themselves into an ever-evolving cycle of production and reproduction. As a child and as a teenager, it was fascinating to watch, especially at the side of a man who was the master at selecting, nurturing, cultivating, preparing, and planning for the long term. He knew it was not a quick fix process; that the true organic gardener took his/her time and made sure everything was part of a process that completed the entire system.

The parallels between organic gardening and Catholic school *development* are quite remarkable. On the wrong side of the row, many in the *development* and/or *advancement* world think it is all about money. They want the quick fix. They want to mail out that direct mail newsletter with a brochure and pledge card and get that money back. They want to go ahead and launch that capital campaign by going to the top donors and asking for their dollars without involving and engaging them. They do not see the value of building community with a capital campaign. They expect families to stay on as parents and students in their school without treating them with *customer service*. The list goes on and on.

People need to be nurtured for a lifetime. As Catholic leaders, we need to identify people constantly and work with them and help them find and share their gifts of expertise, time, talent, wisdom, and financial participation. Many people have many different gifts that cannot all be shared at the same time in their lives. For some, the gift of money is not appropriate at certain stages, and yet the gift of expertise and wisdom is, and should be honored just as much as that gift of money.

True Catholic school development is not a smokescreen for money. It is all about identifying, inviting, nurturing, cultivating, and perpetuating a lifelong relationship as a true steward. The seeds of the G-90 corn are not put into the ground and then hundreds of ears picked the next week. There is a lot to the process, and the beautiful part, is that -- if handled correctly -- it should never end. People, like plants, need to be nurtured for a life time.

LET US PRAY

Throughout this book, I have shared several themes that are interwoven into the 25 Lessons. Reduced to its lowest common denominator, Catholic school development is all about engaging people, having the very best processes to make it successful, and realizing it is indeed a ministry that does bring people closer to Christ and Christ closer to people. I believe that the best way to summarize it all can be found in the words of Archbishop Oscar Romero.

THE LONG VIEW

A Prayer by Archbishop Oscar Romero

It helps, now and then, to step back and take the long view.
The Kingdom is not only beyond our efforts,
It is even beyond our vision.
We accomplish in our lifetime only a tiny fraction of
The magnificent enterprise that is God's work.
Nothing we do is complete,
Which is another way of saying that
The Kingdom always lies beyond us.

No statement says all that should be said.
No prayer fully expresses our faith.
No confession brings perfection,
No pastoral visit brings wholeness.
No program accomplishes the church's mission.
No set of goals and objectives includes everything.

This is what we are about.
We plant the seeds that one day will grow.
We water seeds already planted,
Knowing that they hold future promise.
We lay foundations that will need further development.
We provide yeast that produces effects far beyond our capabilities.

We cannot do everything,
And there is a sense of liberation in realizing that.
This enables us to do something,
And to do it very well.
It may be incomplete,
But it is a beginning,
A step along the way,
An opportunity for the Lord's grace to enter
And do the rest.

We may never see the end results,
But that is the difference
Between the master builder and the worker.

We are workers, not master builders,
Ministers, not messiahs.
We are prophets of a future that is not our own.

Amen.

ACKNOWLEDGEMENTS

There are many people to thank who have been an integral part of this journey in Catholic school development. I do want to acknowledge the following people who have guided, supported, encouraged, and contributed.

- To Sister Mary Ann Hardcastle, RSM, who first encouraged me to open a window after a door was closed when my son Dustin died at the age of 5 in 1986 -- she prompted me to move into the ministry of Catholic development
- To Father Jim Manning, Father Denny Hartigan, and Marguerite Celestin who have always believed in and promoted this company, our mission, and our vision
- To Dr. Erik Goldschmidt, ISPD Executive Vice-President, and Dr. Regina Haney, ISPD adjunct associate, for their on-going collaboration and partnership
- To Bernard Dumond, an ISPD associate for 20 years, for all of his dedication to and application of this philosophy, methodology, and processes
- To Joe Therber, Dan Ferris, and Lisa Gadd Guillot for helping proof the book, and for all of their encouragement and keen insight
- To the ISPD National Advisory Board for their willingness to serve as a sounding board and for sharing their best wisdom guiding the future of ISPD
- To my wife Suzy for her unwavering support, along with our daughter Megan, and for their understanding of the days and nights away from home in this world of Catholic consulting
- To my three adult daughters – Lisa, Shannon and Cheri – for their perseverance in charting their unique journeys of success

ABOUT THE AUTHOR

Frank Donaldson is the president of the Institute of School and Parish Development (ISPD) -- a national development consulting firm created to serve Catholic schools, parishes and dioceses in the areas of planning, marketing, enrollment management and resource development. ISPD is headquartered in the Greater New Orleans, LA. Frank is the author of *Catholic School Publications: Unifying the Image*, a publication available through NCEA. He is also the author of *Development Directions*, a monthly Catholic development newsletter with nationwide circulation. Frank is a frequent presenter at national conferences and conventions, including NCEA. In 1988, after 20 years of being an English/Journalism teacher, a development director, and an administrator in Catholic schools, Frank left the classroom and the role of development director and started ISPD.

Mr. Donaldson has spoken, written and consulted extensively throughout the country, and his firm continues to work with hundreds of Catholic institutions, thereby providing a national perspective. For over 25 years, ISPD has facilitated hundreds of long-range planning processes, established numerous development offices, trained hundreds of development directors and raised millions of dollars for Catholic institutions. All of this has been done using ISPD's major theme of operation: *Catholic Development is all about bringing people, process and ministry together to help build the Kingdom of God.* In 25 lessons, Frank shares how to make this theme come alive in your Catholic school.

Frank and his wife Suzy and their daughter Megan reside in Pearl River, LA, and are members of Our Lady of Lourdes Parish. Frank and Suzy, along with many other parish families at OLL, have worked hard in rebuilding the parish after the devastation caused by Hurricane Katrina in 2005. Their daughter Megan is a graduating senior this year from Mount Carmel Academy in New Orleans, LA. In addition, Frank is a graduate of De La Salle High School, and Suzy is a graduate of Mercy Academy.